I always have tried to keep my spiritual ears open for important, new things that the Holy Spirit is saying to the Churches, and through the years I have been permitted to focus in on several of them. As soon as I began hearing Robert Henderson speak on the courts of Heaven I thought that this might be another one of those divine words. Now that he has put his thoughts in writing with Operating in the Courts of Heaven, I am convinced that this revelation is truly a game-changer for those of us intent on advancing God's kingdom. This is one of the most important books you can read for moving ahead in this present season!

C. Peter Wagner, Vice-President
Global Spheres, Inc.

Robert Henderson has a passion and love for the Body of Christ that is awakening God's people everywhere he ministers. Now Robert has a revelation that we need to seriously consider for unlocking God's will for the world. Here is a key that could change your life and set you free.

Harold R. Eberle
Worldcast Ministries

From the first time I heard Robert teach on the Courtroom of Heaven, the paradigms of my ministry have been shaking and shifting. I was fully aware, with our apostolic intercessory work in Texas, of the authority that we carry as kings and priests of the Most High God, but this material ushered me into a whole new realm of understanding and impartation. Whether we are grandpas, pastors, CEOs, mothers, students or a prayer leader over Texas, it is a powerful revelation to know that your destiny (and the destiny of states and nations) has been inscribed on the books that are set before the Judge and King of all of creation. And He has invited us into that courtroom in order to release and decree that destiny into the earth. This book, Operating in the Courts of Heaven, is not just a "must" read, it is a "must" mindset!

Dr. Thomas Schlueter, Coordinator
Texas Apostolic Prayer Network

OPERATING IN THE

COURTS OF

HEAVEN

Granting God the Legal Right to Fulfill His Passion and Answer Our Prayers

ROBERT
HENDERSON

It is with profound gratitude that I dedicate this book to God my Father who is Judge of all. To Jesus my High Priest, Mediator and Intercessor whose sacrifice provides all I need to operate before the Throne of heaven. To Holy Spirit who is my friend and takes all that Jesus did and helps me execute it into place until the verdicts of the cross are seen in the earth.

I also dedicate this book to my wife Mary and her relentless support and belief in me for all these years. May the Lord greatly reward your faithfulness with years of "being kept busy with the joy of your heart." (Ecclesiastes 5:20)

I also dedicate this book to the tireless intercessors, who through their tears are opening the books of heaven. (Revelation 5:1-5) Without you the Courts of Heaven could not operate to see God's will executed into the earth. I pray that this book will be used to inspire all who are weary with a fresh wind. We must have your prayer power to accomplish what God desires in the earth. You have been and will always be the integral part of kingdom expansion. You are absolutely necessary to books being opened and cases being presented in the Courts of Heaven.

Contents

FOREWORD

I don't remember when I have been so excited about a new book! Dr. Peter Wagner calls this "a game changer," and it truly is. It can change the way you see God and His justice system, and cause you to get new answers from your prayers.

We all have mileposts in our lives when we have received a revelation from God that profoundly changed our life. I believe you will receive just such a revelation as you read this book. You and I want our prayers to make a difference, and God wants that too. He wants to answer our prayers, but He must be just and righteous in answering them.

Righteousness and justice are the foundation of His throne (Psalm 89:14), so we need to have a revelation of those two principles to understand how God's Kingdom works and to get the answers that we and God want. We have operated in these principles when we received answered prayers, but we probably didn't realize what was happening and why.

Dr. Wagner has stated that "the reports that I get from the Heartland Apostolic Prayer Network (hapn.us) are the most tangible measurable results of high level prayer and spiritual warfare that I have heard yet in my life," but it took Robert's teaching to give me a better understanding of why what we did worked and how to make it better.

I have read the book and listened several times to Robert's

teaching CDs on the court system of Heaven and marveled at his insights. We will be buying copies of the book to give to each of the over 100 state and international leaders of the HAPN that I lead because we must get this understanding on how to get more tangible results from our prayers to change our lives, our families, and our nations.

As you study this book, please let the Holy Spirit give you His great grace to revolutionize the results you get from your prayers.

Dr. John M. Benefiel
Presiding Apostle – Heartland Apostolic Prayer Network
Founder and Senior Pastor – Church on the Rock,
Oklahoma City

Introduction

Most people I know believe intensely in prayer. Even those who would not consider themselves Christians, actually believe in prayer—especially in times of trouble, trauma and tribulation. Yet, even with this strong belief in prayer there is still a great deal of frustration concerning how it operates and what we need to do to see our prayers answered. We have all found this frustration at the lack of answers to our prayers to be real and at times confusing.

Some, in an attempt to put a positive spin on the whole issue of God's response to it, have said that God answers all prayers. Sometimes His answer is 'Yes', and we get what we are petitioning Him for. Sometimes His answer is 'No', because He knows better than we do what we need. At other times, His answer is 'Wait', because it is a timing issue. As much as I believe that this is at times correct, I believe it to be too trite and simple an answer. I have watched people pray prayers that I knew were in agreement with God's will, heart and timing, and yet the desired answer did not come. I watched these unanswered prayers result in relationships being destroyed, businesses going under and even premature deaths occurring. Devastating consequences took place because there appeared to be no answer from Heaven.

So what is the problem, or better yet what is the solution? Why does Heaven sometimes remain silent when we pray from the earnestness of our hearts? I believe that the Lord has unveiled, at the very least, a partial answer to this dilemma. The answer is found in where the spiritual activity called prayer is actually taking place.

Prayer, at its very core, is where we insert ourselves into a spiritual conflict. Prayer is not just an asking or petitioning of God for some things. When we pray, we engage the Lord Himself, but we are also engaging powers of darkness that want to resist us in our prayer activity. We see this in the book of Daniel. Daniel is interceding, asking God for understanding regarding the Scriptures. Satan does not want this knowledge released to Daniel and high powers of darkness seek to stop him receiving the answer to his prayers. After 21 days, Daniel finally receives the answer to his prayer and also gains understanding of why the answer took so long to come through. Daniel 10:12-14.

> Then he said to me, "Do not fear, Daniel, for from the first day that you set your heart to understand, and to humble yourself before your God, your words were heard; and I have come because of your words. But the prince of the kingdom of Persia withstood me twenty-one days; and behold, Michael, one of the chief princes, came to help me, for I had been left alone there with the kings of Persia. Now I have come to make you understand what will happen to your people in the latter days, for the vision refers to many days yet to come" (Daniel 10:12-14).

Daniel's prayer engaged God but also engaged the devil and his forces. My point is simply that prayer is almost always about a conflict. Daniel's words stirred Heaven, but also stirred up hell. When we pray we are entering a conflict. We are moving the powers of heaven for God's kingdom will to be done, but we are also engaging the forces of darkness that are resisting that will from being done. This is the power of our words that are directed toward the Lord.

The Apostle Paul talks about this conflict in many of his writings. In 1 Corinthians 9:26 Paul speaks of "one who beats the air" but doesn't land the blows.

> Therefore I run thus: not with uncertainty. Thus I fight: not as one who beats the air (1 Corinthians 9:26).

Paul says he doesn't run with uncertainty, yet we certainly have. We participate in spiritual activities wondering if any of it is doing anything in the unseen realm. He then goes on to say that he doesn't fight as one who beats the air. This is a reference to 'shadow boxing'. Shadow boxing is a training method to build stamina and perfect the art of punching. Shadow boxing is for the gym, for training. It is not something you do in the ring with a real opponent opposite you! When there is a real opponent, real blows need to be landed and damage done to the adversary that is trying to knock you out. If you shadow box in a real match, you will simply wear yourself out and not do any real damage to your opponent. You can be sure he will take advantage of your weakened position, knock you out and win the match.

I speak about this from experience. I was a Junior High student in Texas, and our PE teacher decided that we would have a boxing lesson. I remember the mats being put down and each student taking his turn against an opponent on the mats. I found myself matched up against one of the worst athletes in the school. I was an average athlete, definitely better than my opponent. (That's my assessment of it anyway and I'm sticking to it.) We took our position on the mats, facing each other with our gloves in their right position, as we had been instructed, and we began to punch. I don't really remember what happened, other than as I punched, I threw a wild 'haymaker' of a punch that left my jaw completely exposed. My opponent (the non-athlete) saw it and delivered a left hook that landed perfectly. The next thing I knew, I was lying on my back with all the other guys commenting very vocally on what had just happened to me (the better athlete). I was extremely embarrassed and ashamed. This happened because I was wild in my boxing approach and I didn't know how to land my blows.

This is what many Christians are experiencing. They are throwing punch after punch at an unseen opponent, but landing none of them. The problem is that we are discouraged, faint-hearted and would like to just quit. We are wearing ourselves out. But please don't quit. There are answers to the whole realm of unanswered prayers. Let me give you a clue concerning this mystery before we move on in this book.

If we are to get unanswered prayers answered, we must first rightly discern where the conflict is in which we find ourselves. Most teachers on prayer and spiritual warfare teach that we are on a battlefield. I have come to believe deeply that, at the least, initially our prayers are in the courtroom of Heaven and we need to learn how to operate there if we are to get answers released and unlocked.

The protocol of a battlefield will not work in a courtroom and neither will the protocol of a courtroom work on a battlefield. These are two different arenas and we must discover where we are in prayer if we are to be effective. When we come off the battlefield and get into the courtroom and learn to function there, verdicts come out of the realms of God's throne that put in place the cry of our hearts. We must know how to be a part of the legal process of Heaven that grants God the legal right to fulfill His passion on our behalf and in the Earth. This is what this book is about. Don't be faint-hearted, answers are on the way!

1

Where is the Conflict?

Several years ago I was chosen for jury duty. The case was an armed robbery of a convenience store. The young man on trial was one who supposedly was the 'look out' for this robbery. The deciding factor for us as the jury, was his actions, movements and countenance as he was caught on the surveillance camera. He was definitely guilty even though he claimed that he didn't know that the man he was with was going to rob the store when they went in. The problem was that the camera showed a different story. We placed the young man on probation for the sake of his young wife and children so he could have another chance and not go to prison.

All this activity took place in a courtroom where a verdict was rendered. There was no yelling, screaming or physical wrestling. That would have been completely out of order in these proceedings. Everything that was done was about presenting evidence, making a request, answering accusations and other legal processes. The result was a verdict rendered that was consistent with the petitions that were being offered. Justice was served.

I am convinced that prayer is an activity that takes place in the courtroom of Heaven. There are petitions, accusations, arguments and evidence presented in the courts of Heaven just as there are in the courts on Earth. And just as there is protocol in a natural courtroom, there is protocol in the courtroom of

Heaven. As a member of that jury, it would have been illegal and against the protocol of the courtroom if I were to have pulled out a sword and begun to shout out my opinion about the case. Everyone would have thought I was crazy and I probably would have been arrested because I had not observed the protocol of the court. In the same way, Heaven's courts also have a spiritual protocol that should be observed.

I believe, through Scripture, that the place of the initial conflict is in a courtroom and not on a battlefield. The first place of intercession should be in the courtroom of Heaven. It is there that we must first win our verdicts before going out to win on the battlefield.

The problem is that most Christians believe that when they pray they are on a battlefield. They rush into a conflict without securing a verdict from Heaven. This is a critical mistake that has caused us to experience defeat, chaos, backlash from satanic forces and even destruction in our lives. We rush into places of prayer only to see things get worse rather than better. This is because we stir things up on a battlefield without first having established a legal precedent to be there. I have heard people say that the worsened situation is a sign that something is moving. It's moving alright, just in the wrong direction. Imagine if military leaders applied this 'wisdom'. When experiencing defeat at the hands of the enemy, we just keep on fighting, keep sending our soldiers onto the battlefield to sacrifice their lives in a war we are hoping to win. It is a ridiculous strategy.

Many times it seems prayer and what is called spiritual warfare, is approached with the mindset of General George Custer, who led his troops into a massacre by Native Americans. As a result of his ignorance, arrogance and disregard for proper military strategy, a large part of the United States Calvary was ambushed and destroyed at Little Big Horn. As sad an event as this is in American history, Christians repeat it over and over in their own prayer lives. They keep rushing in and yelling at the devil, making decrees and offering up prayers that do more to stir up demonic forces than dismantle them. All of this happens because no legal precedent has been gained from the Throne of God. As a result no answers come from Heaven and we experience casualties rather than victories. What absurdity! Isn't there a better way to do this with the right results? I say 'Yes!' The answer is to move off the battlefield and into the courtroom of Heaven.

In Revelation 19:11 we see how Jesus Himself approaches this.

> Now I saw Heaven opened, and behold, a white horse. And He who sat on him was called Faithful and True, and in righteousness He judges and makes war (Revelation 19:11).

The first thing we must see is that Heaven is open. This means that there is revelation and things that we need to discern in the Heavenly realm. Prayer and warfare should not be a shot in the dark. We should be able to pinpoint the things that need to be dealt with and touch them with accuracy. We must be able to pray within the will of God. We CAN find the needle in the haystack when Heaven is open and revelation is flowing. John the Apostle said if we ask anything according to His will then we have the petition that we are asking of Him. (1 John 5:14-15) One of the critical steps to effective prayer is understanding the will of God and praying in agreement with that will. I will deal more extensively about how this is done in a later chapter.

The main thing I want to point out in Revelation 19:11 is that Jesus, Who is faithful and true, judges in righteousness and makes war. Notice the order of this wording. This is very important. Jesus judges, then makes war. When the Bible speaks of 'judging', it is speaking of judicial activity. There is a decision and a verdict being rendered concerning a situation, petition and/or request. That activity is being judged and there is a legal precedent that is being established concerning it. Out of that judicial activity which is flowing from the courts of Heaven, war is made. We must learn to only make war based on judgments, decisions and verdicts that are received out of the courts of Heaven. To try to make war without a verdict and judgment from the court of Heaven is to suffer defeat and even satanic backlash because we have no legal footing to be there or be engaging in such activity. On the other hand, if we can get legal renderings concerning a situation in place, then we can march onto the battlefield and win every time. The problem has been that we have tried to win on the battlefield without legal verdicts from Heaven backing us up. We must learn how to get these verdicts and judgments in place so answers can come to our prayers and the Kingdom cause of Christ can land on the Earth.

Jesus and the Courts of Heaven

Jesus set prayer in a courtroom setting. In Scripture we see references made to warfare and the battlefield. Yet in Jesus' teaching on prayer in Matthew 6 and Luke 11, Jesus never placed prayer on a battlefield. He spoke of prayer as flowing from the relationship to a father. He spoke of prayer as a friend approaching a friend. Yet when dealing with the question of how to pray, Jesus never said we were on a battlefield. He did however place prayer in a courtroom or judicial setting. In Luke 18:1-8, Jesus speaks of a widow who is seeking justice from a courtroom.

Then He spoke a parable to them, that men always ought to pray and not lose heart, saying: "There was in a certain city a judge who did not fear God nor regard man. Now there was a widow in that city; and she came to him, saying, 'Get justice for me from my adversary.' And he would not for a while; but afterward he said within himself, 'Though I do not fear God nor regard man, yet because this widow troubles me I will avenge her, lest by her continual coming she weary me.'" Then the Lord said, "Hear what the unjust judge said. And shall God not avenge His own elect who cry out day and night to Him, though He bears long with them? I tell you that He will avenge them speedily. Nevertheless, when the Son of Man comes, will He really find faith on the earth?" (Luke 18:1-8)

Clearly, Jesus is declaring that when we pray, we are entering a courtroom. If this widow could get an answer and a verdict from an unjust judge through her persistent activity in a court, how much more shall we gain answers as the elect of God before the Righteous Judge of all. I think it is very interesting that Jesus spoke this parable so people would not give up on prayer. We must realize that a lack of results does not mean we need to put more effort into something. More effort without additional wisdom usually produces tiredness, fatigue and weariness. What we need is not more effort necessarily, but to learn secrets. Striving produces frustration while the revelation of secrets produces fruit. The mindset that we have had in the Church is flawed. What we are doing is not producing results, but we think that if we can just keep doing it long enough, loud enough or hard enough, then somehow, magically, something different will happen.

Before I entered the ministry, I worked at a meat packing plant where there were many illegal workers. This was before the government began to crack down on this practice. I was in the maintenance crew and was responsible for helping to keep the machines running and production at its maximum. The problem was that some of these workers didn't care what they damaged in the process of doing their job. For instance, one day as a piece of equipment was being moved from one place to another, it had to go through a door. As they were pushing this machinery through the door, it became jammed and wouldn't move. Instead of going around on the other side and seeing why it was stuck, they just called for more people to come and push harder. The result was they 'broke' it free, but damaged other things that were in the way. Their philosophy was the same as many in the Church. Why check and see why something is not working and stuck, when you can just use more effort? More effort is not always the answer. Many times the answer is the discovering of secrets through revelation that actually brings about a breakthrough with less effort and produces greater results. If we have done the same thing for years and it hasn't improved, but in fact it has become even worse, maybe we should investigate. Someone once defined this as the definition of insanity. They said insanity is doing the same thing over and over and expecting something different to happen. We do not need more effort and striving, we need to discover secrets that unlock new dimensions that produce new results.

This is why Jesus was speaking this parable. He was unlocking a secret that prayer is activity in a courtroom. When the widow wanted justice, she went to the courtroom and not the battlefield. She realized she didn't need to march onto a battlefield and yell at her adversary. She simply needed a verdict from the court. In fact she didn't even address her adversary. This parable never mentions her even speaking to him. She spoke only to the judge. When this widow kept on with her pleas before the unjust judge, he finally gave in and granted her request and she received a just verdict in her situation. She understood that if the Judge rendered a legal verdict, any power of the adversary was demolished and she won. Once this was in place her adversary had to bow the knee to the rendering of the court.

This is so for us as well. Any adversary in the spirit realm that is resisting God's Kingdom purpose for us will bow the knee to verdicts from the court of Heaven. We have no need to yell, scream or even curse our foe. All we need is a legal precedent based on a verdict from Heaven and the fight is over. We then simply put into place the verdict that has been set down. This is where decrees come, but only after legality has been established. I will get into this more in a later chapter. I want us to notice specifically Luke 18:8.

> I tell you that He will avenge them speedily (Luke 18:8).

I have watched and witnessed that when I moved off the battlefield and into the courtroom of Heaven, answers came for me that I had prayed years for. All my warring, crying, yelling and petitioning had not brought answers from Heaven. But, when I began to learn how to navigate the courts of Heaven what had never happened before, happened immediately and quickly. My adversaries were silenced and I was avenged 'speedily'.

As with most families, my family does not live in a perfect world. I hope yours does, but mine doesn't. Mary and I have raised six children. I have said often that while they were growing up, we were never bored! We were confused at times, but never bored! There was definitely plenty of activity and life in our home. We have watched all of the children transition into great adults. They all love God, fear Him and honor Mary and I greatly.

This has not been without periods of wrong choices as they struggled to discover their identities. In fact, one of our daughters went through a very short period of rebellious activity. That period was long enough however to end with her being pregnant without being married. I love what a prophet friend of mine says. He declares, "It is not a sin to be pregnant without being married." This statement usually stuns people. After all, how could any legitimate man or woman of God say such a thing? He then continues, "The sin was the fornication that led to the pregnancy. The baby in the womb is not a sin." I love it. Not because of any justification in our own personal circumstance, but because it strikes at the malicious judgment that is so often in the Church concerning such situations. God is a God of forgiveness and mercy. Whether it was our daughter or someone else's, there is forgiveness and redemption for whoever will repent for the activity that brought on the pregnancy outside of marriage. After the repentance then there is a joyous expectation of the child that will be born into the Earth completely blessed by our loving God who is our Father. This is what has happened in our family. Our grandson is a joy to our lives and the whole clan. We cannot imagine life without him.

One of the first places where I saw activity in the courts of Heaven bring a verdict was concerning this grandson. The biological father in the situation decided after five years that he wanted to be back in this child's life. There had been no support of any kind from him up until then. The character of the father was not one which we felt would be a good influence on our grandson. He had a criminal record, several DUI's, plus a couple of assault convictions. It was not a good situation. Yet here he was, wanting visitation rights and the right to take our grandson out of State for extended visitations with his family. Our daughter was greatly perplexed and worried about what the natural courts would do.

It came time for the case to go before a judge. The attorney for my daughter was guarded because he didn't know which way the judge would go. We lived in Colorado Springs and it is a military town. Cases such as these go before the courts regularly because of people who are in the military. They get divorced and one party will be transferred to other regions around the world. It is not uncommon for the courts to allow visitation rights, so a child can be taken out of State and be with the other parent. This is what my daughter thought would happen and this was of great concern to her. But she didn't know her dad (me) had discovered a higher court that could be appealed to.

On the day of the earthly court date, I went into the courts of Heaven, silenced the accuser (we will get to that later) and petitioned the court of Heaven for a verdict and judgment in our daughter and ultimately our grandson's favor. I had some other prophetic people helping me sense what was going on. I very clearly heard and discerned that the court of Heaven had rendered the verdict we were looking for.

My daughter went to the earthly court later that morning. As the judge listened to the evidence, he prepared to render his judgment. He then spoke to the biological father and said these words, "Young man, here's what we are going to do. Whatever the mother wants us to do is what we are going to do. Are you fine with this?" My daughter, her attorney and the biological father were flabbergasted. My daughter's attorney actually took her outside and asked her if she realized what had just happened. He said that this never happens and he was beside himself at the turn of events.

The reason for this activity and verdict was because a higher court, the court of Heaven had already rendered a verdict and the earthly court simply played it out. I have watched this happen in several actual court cases. I have also seen results like this over and over as we have asked Heaven to render verdicts to set Kingdom purposes in place. This principle and awareness is a very powerful thing. The more we learn to present our case in the courts of Heaven, the more we get legal precedents in place that allow us victory on the battlefield every time. Without it we lose and suffer the consequences. Let's learn to go to court!

2

The Books of Heaven

If we really want to get results from the courts of Heaven, we need to know how to operate within these courts. Lawyers go to school for years to learn how to operate within our judicial systems. They learn to speak the language of the courts. Just as they must know how to address the court, present cases and briefs, so we too must learn how to present things before Heaven's court. One of the greatest mysteries to this process is understanding the books or scrolls that are in Heaven.

Daniel 7:10 tells us that there are books or scrolls in Heaven that must be opened before the court of Heaven goes into session. Once the courts of Heaven are seated the books are opened and the court appears to come to session.

> A fiery stream issued
> And came forth from before Him.
> A thousand thousands ministered to Him;
> Ten thousand times ten thousand stood before Him.
> The court was seated,
> And the books were opened (Daniel 7:10).

From this Scripture, we can clearly see that an understanding of 'the books' is foundational to court activity that allows God's Kingdom purposes to be done. But what are these books and what is written in them?

Types of Books

Psalm 139:16 tells us that each person has a book in Heaven.

> Your eyes saw my substance, being yet unformed.
> And in Your book they all were written,
> The days fashioned for me,
> When as yet there were none of them (Psalm 139:16).

God wrote down in a book the destiny and Kingdom purpose for each of our lives. God 'saw' us in our fleshly form in the Earth, before we ever existed. He saw our days. Not just the number of them, but He saw the activities in them and what we would accomplish in our life. Our individual book is a written record of all that God planned for us and the Kingdom impact He has destined for our lives. Every person ever born has a book written about them. The battle is to get what is in the book to manifest on the Earth.

Even Jesus had a book. Hebrews 10:5-7 tells us that Jesus had a volume of the book that He came into the Earth to fulfill.

> Therefore, when He came into the world, He said:
> "Sacrifice and offering You did not desire,
> But a body You have prepared for Me. In burnt offerings and sacrifices for sin You had no pleasure.
> Then I said, 'Behold, I have come—
> In the volume of the book it is written of Me To do Your will, O God'" (Hebrews 10:5-7).

There is a book in Heaven that chronicled what Kingdom purpose Jesus would fulfill in the Earth. Jesus came with a passion and a commitment to complete what had been written in the books of Heaven about Him. This is interesting because John 1:14 says that Jesus is the Word made flesh.

> And the Word became flesh and dwelt among us, and we beheld His glory, the glory as of the only begotten of the Father, full of grace and truth (John 1:14).

In other words, Jesus was the Word sent out of Heaven to be born in the flesh. His physical birth allowed what was written in the book of Heaven to be made manifest in the flesh. He then spent the next thirty three and a half years of His life fulfilling what had been written in His book.

Anything God-ordained is first written in a book or scroll in Heaven. It must be sent out of Heaven and birthed into the Earth realm before it can become flesh. This is what happened to Jesus, but also to us and anything else that is ever 'born' into the Earth realm. So it could be said that before we came into the Earth, we were a word written in a scroll. When we were born into the Earth, we began the process of living out our Kingdom purpose as it was written in Heaven in our book. This is why Ephesians 2:10 says that we are His workmanship.

> For we are His workmanship, created in Christ Jesus for good works, which God prepared beforehand that we should walk in them (Ephesians 2:10).

The word workmanship in the Greek means a poem. We are God's poem that was written down in Heaven that has now entered Earth. We are a poem with a point. Our lives carry a message that is creative and life giving. Notice that this poem was written down and the works we are to do were planned beforehand. We were a 'scroll' in Heaven with poetic power that has now entered the Earth to cause the writings of Heaven to become flesh.

There are not just books about individuals. There are also books about churches, apostolic networks, businesses, ministries, cities, states, regions and nations. Heaven is full of books. Anything that is purposed of the Lord will begin as a book in Heaven. The Apostle John while in Heaven was given a book that he was commanded to eat. This book was about nations. Revelation 10:8-11 shows an angel with a little book that had the destinies of nations in it.

> Then the voice which I heard from Heaven spoke to me again and said, "Go, take the little book which is open in the hand of the angel who stands on the sea and on the earth." So I went to the angel and said to him, "Give me the little book." And he said to me, "Take and eat it; and it will make your stomach bitter, but it will be as sweet as honey in your mouth." Then I took the little book out of the angel's hand and ate it, and it was as sweet as honey in my mouth. But when I had eaten it, my stomach became bitter. And he said to me, "You must prophesy again about many peoples, nations, tongues, and kings" (Revelation 10:8-11).

John was instructed to take the book and eat it. This book was from Heaven and was about the future and Kingdom purpose of nations. We know this because the result of John eating the book was the ability to prophesy to peoples, nations, tongues and kings. It was going to become the job of the Apostle John to prophesy out of the books what God had said about these nations. When John would prophesy from the books, it allowed court sessions to begin. Revelation 19:10 tells us the "testimony of Jesus is the spirit of prophecy."

> And I fell at his feet to worship him. But he said to me, "See that you do not do that! I am your fellow servant, and of your brethren who have the testimony of Jesus. Worship God! For the testimony of Jesus is the spirit of prophecy" (Revelation 19:10).

The word testimony means to give judicial witness. Jesus, from His position as our High Priest and Mediator, is testifying in our behalf in the courts. Notice that this testimony becomes a spirit of prophecy in our mouths. When we prophesy, we are not just speaking to the earthly realm, but we are in fact picking up and discerning the present testimony of Jesus in the courts of Heaven.

We are agreeing with and echoing the testimony of Jesus. This grants Heaven the right testimony to render verdicts in our behalf and the Kingdom purposes of God even in nations.

Where do the Books Come From?

These books that are in Heaven came into being from the 'counsel' of the Lord. Jeremiah 23:18 says there was a 'counsel' of the Lord.

> For who has stood in the counsel of the Lord,
> And has perceived and heard His word?
> Who has marked His word and heard it? (Jeremiah 23:18)

This word counsel in Hebrew is *sod*. It means *a company of persons in session, to consult, or a secret*. It comes from the Hebrew word *yasad*, which means to *sit down together, to settle and consult*. Clearly God has counsels that are held in Heaven for the purpose of planning future Kingdom events. Genesis 1:26 says that the Godhead had a counsel about the creating and forming of man.

> Then God said, "Let Us make man in Our image, according to Our likeness; let them have dominion over the fish of the sea, over the birds of the air, and over the cattle, over all the earth and over every creeping thing that creeps on the earth" (Genesis 1:26).

Notice that God said *Let Us*. In other words there was discussion in the counsel of Heaven concerning the formation of man in the image and likeness of God. From this counsel, books were written about the destiny of Earth, man and God's creation. What was written in these books from the counsel of the Lord is what we are seeking to birth into a flesh demonstration.

In 2 Timothy 1:9 Paul is exhorting Timothy to fulfill what was planned before time began.

> "...who has saved us and called us with a holy calling, not according to our works, but according to His own purpose and grace which was given to us in Christ Jesus before time began," (2 Timothy 1:9).

Notice that purpose and grace were given to Paul and Timothy *before time began*. This is really interesting. This means that purpose and grace have been waiting on us to discover them from before time began. Purpose is what is written in the books of Heaven about them and grace was the empowerment to bring it into the realities of the Earth realm. This was given to them *before time began or in the counsel of the Lord.*

To understand this we must know that before we existed in the earth there was a book about us in heaven. From the counsel of the Lord, the Lord made decisions concerning us. The giving and receiving of counsel is for the purpose of arriving at decisions. It is amazing to realize that God Himself not only is the Counselor (Isaiah 9:6) but receives counsel as well. We see this in Isaiah chapter 6 and verse 8 where Isaiah is cleansed from what is polluting him and then hears a "counseling" session in Heaven.

"Also I heard the voice of the Lord, saying: "Whom shall I send, And who will go for Us?" Then I said, "Here *am* I! Send me" (Isaiah 6:8).

Notice that the Lord is asking for "counsel" here. He wants input as to whom shall be used to carry His message into the earth. Isaiah volunteers as he is "eavesdropping" on this "counseling session" in heaven. Clearly from this counsel, a decision was made to allow Isaiah the right and privilege to run with this message of the Lord. I believe that before the Lord releases life-impacting messages, church altering truths and/or planet changing revelation there is counsels in heaven. These counsels are for the purpose of deciding who will carry these messages forth. Once these decisions are made, truth is revealed to the ones chosen for this assignment. This word declared has impacting effect into the spheres intended. It is quite interesting to get glimpses into the working of heaven/the spirit realm. There is much more happening there sometimes than what we are aware of.

Once decisions are made in heaven, then decisions must be made in the earth. From the counsel of the Lord, the books of heaven are written and assignments are delegated. At this point we as people of the earth must decide if we will obey what heaven intends. Jesus spoke of this in the parable of the two sons. In Matthew chapter 21 and verses 28 through 31 Jesus talks of two sons that a father sends to work in a vineyard.

> "But what do you think? A man had two sons, and he came to the first and said, 'Son, go, work today in my vineyard.'
> He answered and said, 'I will not,' but afterward he regretted it and went.
> Then he came to the second and said likewise. And he answered and said, 'I *go*, sir,' but he did not go. Which of the two did the will of *his* father?" They said to Him, "The first." Jesus said to them, "Assuredly, I say to you that tax collectors and harlots enter the kingdom of God before you" (Matthew 21: 28-31).

The first son spoken of said he would go but didn't. The second son said he wouldn't obey but later repented and went. Jesus point was the second one did the will of God because of his repentance. The first one looked like he would obey but didn't. There were decisions made on earth concerning the desire of heaven. Once decisions are made in heaven, we in the earth are then faced with decisions. We must choose correctly to be in agreement with the desire of God that is coming from decisions made in His counsel. When decisions in earth agree with the decisions in heaven powerful things occur.

The other significant issue here is that it would be wonderful if the first son had said yes to the father and fulfilled his desire.

This would have been the ultimate. Yet it was the son who at first rebelled but later repented that actually did the father's will. The Lord is so very merciful. Even when we get it wrong initially, He grants us more opportunities to fulfill what our ultimate purpose is. To completely miss the intent and desire of God for our lives requires sustained rebellion in the face of God's faithful dealings with us. We are granted opportunity after opportunity to decide in favor of the decisions of heaven. May we not squander the mercies and grace of God extended to us. For those who do His will, it is because He works in us by His grace to bring us to an agreement with Him. In Philippians chapter 2 and verse 13 we see this.

"for it is God who works in you both to will and to
do for *His* good pleasure" (Philippians 2:13).

His grace produces in those who will allow it an agreement with His will and pleasure. We must choose agreement with Him. When we do, His grace changes our hearts to agree with Him.

Not everyone lives out what was established in the counsels of the Lord and then written in the books. We don't have to, but it is our job to discover and fulfill what is there and bring it to Earth in natural forms. This is what we will be judged on in the hereafter. Our judgment will not be so much about this sin or that sin. Our judgment will be based on how closely we lived our lives to what is written in the books of Heaven. Not to live our lives out in agreement with the books of Heaven is to waste our time here. We may get to spend eternity in Heaven, but we will not have fulfilled His Kingdom agenda for our life and times here on Earth.

Mary and I have six children. They are all grown now. Well let's just say they are all of legal age and are all over 20 years old. That would be more truthful. When we had four children and the youngest, Hope, was five, Mary was especially happy because Hope was about to start kindergarten. This would mean that for the first time in many years she would be able to have several hours a day when kids were not at home. We were approaching that wonderful time when this would happen. I will never forget Mary and I going on a trip to a borrowed condo on a golf course. We had ditched the kids somewhere and were going to get some time alone for the first time in a long time. There were several other couples that were on this trip. The condo that we were in didn't have enough bedrooms therefore Mary and I were sleeping on a mattress on the floor. I remember waking up the first morning and lying beside Mary. She looked at me and said, "I need to tell you something." I thought in this wonderful moment of peace and quiet, when it was just the two of us, that she was going to tell me how wonderful I was and how much she loved me and loved our life together. She then blurted out the words I had heard before, "I'm pregnant." I don't know what I said, but it was probably something like, "You're kidding, right?"

But no! It was absolutely true. There went our plans down the drain and at least five more years of kids at home before this one would get into school. The truth is that Micah and his brother Mark, the sixth one (yes, we even had another one after this), have been great blessings in our life. But the event I want to tell you about happened when Micah, this fifth one that we were not expecting, was ten years old.

One night Mary had a dream. In the dream she was told that Micah was supposed to have been born to another couple named Mike and Carol (not the Brady Bunch). Carol had been killed in a car wreck and therefore what God intended to do through them could not occur. Micah couldn't be born into the

Earth. The problem was that God needed Micah born so he could fulfill his Kingdom purpose for God's will to be done in the Earth. God chose Mary and I to have Micah instead of the other couple, because Micah had to be born. Isn't that wild? Yet I believe it with every fiber of my being.

It was foreordained in the counsels of Heaven, a book was written as a result of this counsel about and for Micah and God chose us as a second option to get Micah into the Earth. When we received this understanding about Micah's birth, I jokingly said, "God must have been scraping the bottom of the barrel on this one to have to entrust Micah to us!" Actually, I am quite honored that the Lord would entrust one that He needed in the Earth to us. His grace is sufficient for us to impact Micah in the way that is necessary for him to fulfill his book from Heaven.

All of us are a product of the counsel of the Lord. The Lord thought about each one of us and wrote a book about our lives out of that counsel. Each of us has been birthed into the Earth so that His word can be made flesh and what was written in our scrolls can be fulfilled. When this is done, Kingdom influence comes to the Earth and Kingdom cultures that look like Heaven are revealed.

Manifesting the Books

To really understand the "counsel of the Lord" and the books of Heaven we must look at Romans 8:29-30. This passage unveils a five-step process of how to identify and birth the intentions of God into the Earth.

> For whom He foreknew, He also predestined to be conformed to the image of His Son, that He might be the firstborn among many brethren. Moreover

whom He predestined, these He also called; whom He called, these He also justified; and whom He justified, these He also glorified (Romans 8:29-30).

In this Scripture, Paul lists the 5 steps - *foreknew, predestined, called, justified and glorified.* To operate in the courts of Heaven and get what is in Heaven into the Earth, we must understand these stages.

Foreknowledge speaks of that which occurred in the counsel of the Lord. In this counsel decisions were made about destinies in the Earth. This includes individuals, cities, states, businesses and all the way up to nations. There were conclusions that were arrived at concerning what part of God's Kingdom agenda each would fulfill. From the counsel of the Lord, there was a foreknowing of us. This all occurred *before time began.* Once these decisions were made, they were then written down in a book. Once they were written in a book in Heaven, it became a predestined thing. This is the next stage that Paul spoke of.

From the counsel of the Lord (foreknowledge), God then wrote in a book the decisions made that would be our Kingdom reason for existence on the planet. Anything that has a Kingdom purpose has a book in Heaven about it. The books of Heaven contain the Kingdom purposes of God. I like to say that if there isn't a book about it in Heaven, don't waste your time on it. We should only involve ourselves in that which is important to Heaven. If it is important in Heaven, there is a book about it.

Being **predestined** has nothing to do with us not having a choice or a will. In fact we can have a predestined plan for our lives and not fulfill it. Each person born into the Earth arrived with a predestined plan concerning their life. They have a book in Heaven about them. We can either choose to discover what is in the books about us or disregard it and go our own way.

It is each ones individual responsibility to discover what was predestined about them and written in the books of Heaven.

Remember that Paul told Timothy in 2 Timothy 1:9 that purpose and grace were given to them before time began. This means that when we find our purpose we will also discover grace that has been apportioned to us for that purpose. This is the chief way we know we have discovered purpose. We realize that in this activity and life ambition there is grace. In other words, you enjoy it, you are good at it, you have success in doing it and others are influenced by your doing of it. It is much like Eric Liddel in the movie "Chariots of Fire" where he chose to honor God by not running on the Sabbath. He said, "When I run, I feel the pleasure of God." This statement reveals that he had discovered, for this season of his life, the purpose for which he was graced. The two stages of foreknowledge and predestination all occurred before time began. They happened in the eternal realm of God and outside the time realm.

The next stage is the **called** stage. This is the stage where we begin to get glimpses of what we were made for. We begin to discover what is written in the books of heaven about us. This is the biggest question that people have. What is written in my book? What is the predestined plan of God for my life? Psalm 40:6-8 gives us some understanding.

> Sacrifice and offering You did not desire; My ears You have opened. Burnt offering and sin offering You did not require. Then I said, "Behold, I come; In the scroll of the book it is written of me. I delight to do Your will, O my God, And Your law is within my heart" (Psalm 40:6-8).

These verses are actually Jesus prophesying over Himself

before He came into the planet. This verse is later picked up and repeated with some minor changes in Hebrews 10:5-7. This is Jesus saying that He has a book in Heaven that He is coming to flesh out in the Earth. Remember that this is our job. We are to flesh out in the Earth what is written in the books of Heaven. Again, John 1:14 says that Jesus was the Word made flesh. In other words, what was written about Him in Heaven in the books, He has come to bring to reality in the Earth.

Notice that Jesus said that in the scroll or volume of the book it was written of Him. He had come to do the will of the Father contained in that book. But then He makes a very powerful statement. In connection to fulfilling what is in the His book, He says, "*And Your law is within my heart*". So whatever is written in your book in Heaven is also written in your heart. If you want to discover what is in your book, look in your heart. What are your interests, desires, aspirations, longings and passions? These are clues to what is in your book in Heaven. Many times our lives become so cluttered and busy that we need the Holy Spirit to come and unveil for us what is in our hearts. When we discover the passion of our heart, we will begin to discover what is written in our books in Heaven. We will start to have glimpses of what our Kingdom purposes are.

The next stage is the being **justified**. Justified has legal implications. The word means to *be rendered just or innocent*. In other words there are no accusations that can stick. Remember that the devil is the accuser of the brethren who accuses us before God day and night. (Revelation 12:10). The justified stage is where we have been into the courtroom of Heaven and every accusation the devil is using against us is silenced.

Accusations are what the devil uses to keep us from what is written in the books of Heaven about us. This is why so many people are frustrated today. They have an intuitive awareness that they were created for something more than they have become. They sense that something is resisting them from stepping into all they were made for. That which is resisting them is the accusation of the accuser against them in the courts of Heaven. The accuser is presenting evidence to God the Judge of all as to why He cannot legally grant to you what is written in your book. Satan knows that if we get what is in our book, then we will do massive damage to his devilish empire in the Earth. He uses accusations against us to stop us from stepping into all that Heaven has ordained.

He did this to Peter. We will see this clearly as we talk about it in later chapters. Suffice it to say that if we want what is in our books fleshed out in the Earth, the accusations of Satan must be answered. Once this is done then God as Judge of all is free to fulfill His Father's passion toward us and grant what is in the book so heaven's will concerning us can be done.

The fifth and final stage mentioned is being **glorified**. Being glorified is not talking about going to Heaven. It is speaking about us fully stepping into all that is written in the books of Heaven about us. We begin to "live the dream." We live the dream that God had about us before time begin. This has been called the convergence point. It is where everything we have gone through, good or bad, works together to propel us into our ultimate destiny.

We see this in the life of Joseph where he was in his father's house, but then sold into slavery by jealous brothers. He ended up ruling over the household of Potiphar. Then he was cast into prison unjustly, after which he was promoted from this most unlikely place to Prime Minister of Egypt. He became the preserver of life that God had destined him to be as it was written in the books of Heaven. All of these things worked together and converged together to prepare and get

Joseph to his appointed place. He then, from his glorified position, had the Kingdom impact that was predestined by God that he was to have. The reaching of the convergence point of our lives can be costly and expensive but worth it. Not only do we find the ultimate satisfaction that we were built for, but God gets His Kingdom purpose fulfilled through us.

The most critical stage of this process for individuals all the way to nations, is being justified. Once we maneuver our ways through the courts of Heaven and get legal things arranged, God can freely then grant to us the passion of His heart.

In the next chapter we will talk about the court activity of Heaven that allows what is written in the books of Heaven to come into the Earth realm. There is a great contention regarding this, but when we know how to function in the courts we grant God the legal rights for the word to be made flesh.

3

Contending for the Books

On a trip to Germany, I found myself operating in a Heavenly courtroom setting. The folks that I was ministering with are very skilled at going into the courts of Heaven and getting things legally in place so God's will can be done on the Earth. As we were functioning in this sphere and contending with the powers of darkness over Germany, one of the seer prophets became aware that there was a 'book' that had come into the courtroom. It was tattered, worn and had been through a destructive process. Something had tried to destroy this book. We recognized that this was the book that contained the kingdom purpose of God for Germany. We navigated through the courtroom procedures until we were able to secure the book of Germany that had been taken captive by the demonic principalities. This was good news for the nation of Germany.

Germany, just like any other nation, has a book in Heaven that chronicles what its kingdom purpose is in God's economy. Germany cannot be redeemed to its kingdom purpose until its book is secured, then opened and read into being. When we were able to secure the book legally out of the hands of principalities and powers, we began the journey of accomplishing things in the Heavens. By the way, there was no yelling and screaming at the devil. There was only legal wrangling in the court that allowed us to possess the book of Germany and take it back from satanic powers. This was necessary for Germany to come to a place of redemption and begin the process of becoming a sheep nation.

This is the heart of God for every nation - that they fulfill their destiny as it is written in their book. But in order to fulfill it, they must first lay hold of their book. This is why John was told to eat the scroll or book in Revelation 10:9-11. When he ate the book that had the destinies of nations written in it, he was empowered to prophesy those destinies and reveal them to the nations. And more than that, he could petition for them in the courts of Heaven.

The books in Heaven are absolutely central to the operation of the courts of Heaven. Again, Daniel 7:10 shows us that the court cannot operate until the books are open.

> A fiery stream issued
> And came forth from before Him.
> A thousand thousands ministered to Him;
> Ten thousand times ten thousand stood before Him.
> The court was seated,
> And the books were opened (Daniel 7:10).

Once the court is in session and the books are open, cases can be presented, legal precedents set and the dominion rights of principalities removed from nations. This occurs when we begin to present cases from the revelation we are seeing and understanding out of the books of Heaven. This is why it was so important to get the book of Germany back from the powers of darkness that had taken it captive. Now that we have received the book back, we are able to read prophetically the blueprint of God for the nation. What is written in the book concerning Germany is now closer to being realized than before. There will need to be much more operation in the courts of Heaven, but Germany like any other nation can see its Kingdom purpose fulfilled when we dismantle the legal arguments that allow the powers of darkness to rule. Step by step and piece by piece we take away these legalities and grant God the legal right to fulfill His Kingdom will.

The Word Becomes Flesh

I wanted to use this illustration of what happened in Germany to emphasize that there is a contending for what is in the books. Whether it is on a national level or a personal level, the devil does not want what is in the books to come into reality on the Earth. This is why there were such extreme attempts by satanic powers to keep Jesus out of the Earth. Remember that the devil tried to exterminate the Jewish race several times. This was to remove from the planet the race of people through which Jesus would be born.

Then after He was born, Herod sent out a decree to kill all the babies within Jesus' age range. This was to try to destroy Him. Why was this done and many other things done? What was the purpose? It was to keep the Word from being made flesh (John 1:14). It was to keep what was written about Jesus in the books of Heaven from entering the Earth.

This is true for anything that is written in Heaven. Whether it is nations, churches, businesses, individuals or any other thing, there will be attempts to keep what is in the books from coming into the Earth realm. Satan does not want the word made flesh on any level. Everything that is written in the books about you, nations, Kingdom purposes and God's desires will be contested. The devil does not want what is written in the books to be born into the Earth and be made flesh. It is our job to see this accomplished.

A primary thing I want us to realize is that the conflict for what is in the books is in a courtroom and not on a battlefield. That is why when the court is seated in Daniel 7 the books are then opened. We are not on a battlefield. We are in a courtroom to get God's Kingdom purposes into the Earth. I know I have already said this, but I must continue to emphasize it because we must make this shift in our thinking. The protocol and manner of operation in a courtroom is different from that on a battlefield. We are seeking to get legal things in place for ultimate victory.

Another very important thing we must know about contending for books to come into the Earth realm is that there are varying levels of courts in Heaven. Zechariah 3:7 shows us that the Lord promised Joshua, the High Priest, that if he walked in holiness, he would have a place to walk in the courts of Heaven.

> "Thus says the Lord of hosts: 'If you will walk in
> My ways,
> And if you will keep My command,
> Then you shall also judge My house,
> And likewise have charge of My courts;
> I will give you places to walk
> Among these who stand here (Zechariah 3:7).

This says several very important things to us. First, Joshua was a mortal man that was being granted access and function in the courts of Heaven. I will touch on this more later, but suffice it to say now that what Heaven wants done cannot happen without our involvement. Even though we are physically on Earth, in the spirit we can function in the courts of Heaven and have authority there.

Another thing is that our walk is very important. From our walk or conduct in holiness before the Lord, we gain authority in the courts of Heaven. When we walk in a manner worthy of Him, Heaven recognizes us. So many folks have a misconstrued concept of grace. I thank God for His grace. His grace saves me from my sin, but it also empowers me to live above sin. Titus 2:11-12 tells us that God's real grace not only saves us, but instructs us in forsaking ungodliness and lustful things.

> For the grace of God that brings salvation has appeared to all men, teaching us that, denying ungodliness and worldly lusts, we should live soberly, righteously, and godly in the present age, (Titus 2:11-12)

God's grace will empower me to live in a godly manner in this present age. When I appropriate His grace into my life to live in holiness, I gain authority before the courts of Heaven.

Levels of Courts

The other important thing is that Joshua the High Priest is told that he will have charge of the courts of Heaven. Notice that it is courts plural. This is significant. Even on Earth there are varying levels and types of courts that decide issues. There are small claims courts, criminal courts, civil courts, divorce courts, city courts, district courts, all the way up to the Supreme Court within my nation of America. All these courts have a different function and jurisdiction. These courts function within the sphere that has been granted to them.

In Heaven, there are many different courts that operate. Everyone is not recognized or allowed to operate in all courts. Our operation in the courts of Heaven is determined by the measurement of rule or jurisdiction we have been given. For instance, there are only a handful of attorneys that can present cases in the Supreme Court of the United States. If an attorney that is not recognized comes before the Supreme Court he or she will not be allowed to function there. They will be escorted out or not even allowed in. We must realize this or we can get ourselves into major trouble by trying to operate in a jurisdiction of Heaven that we have not been granted. When we do this, we open ourselves up to satanic assault and backlash. We have stepped outside our realm and our lives and the lives of those joined to us could be put in jeopardy. I will talk more about this in another chapter.

The Throne of Grace

The good news is that there is a court we can operate in, as believers, that is accessible for us all. It is called the Throne of grace. Hebrews 4:16 tells us about this court.

> Let us therefore come boldly to the throne of grace, that we may obtain mercy and find grace to help in time of need (Hebrews 4:16).

Everything we deal with on a personal or family level can be brought to the throne of grace. At this throne or in this court we can obtain mercy and find grace to help in our time of need. I function in this court setting on a regular basis.

The first time I functioned in this court was on behalf of my son, Adam. Adam had gone through a very difficult time. He had been married and had a baby with a girl that decided she didn't want to be in ministry with him. They were youth pastors in the Northwest part of our nation and were very effective in this ministry. Through a series of events they moved back to where they had both grown up. She became involved with her 'old friends' and her family. The result was she left Adam and took the baby with her. Adam was not without fault or blame, but nothing warranted this kind of decision being made. The result was a divorce that separated Adam from everything he loved. He didn't want the divorce, but was powerless to stop it. This caused Adam to go into a place of deep depression. I tried everything over the course of the next couple of years to get him out of it. Nothing worked. He would go to work from 3 p.m. until 11 p.m. every day then come home, go to his room and play online video games all night. This was his way of dealing with the pain and loss that he had suffered. I would try and talk to him, encourage him and motivate him to come out of this place. There would be no response from him. He wasn't mean or nasty, he was just lifeless.

In addition to everything I have mentioned, I prayed vigilantly for Adam every day. My attitude towards him and this situation was that brute force in prayer would get the job done. This was my attitude in prayer about everything. I figured if it didn't move, it just needed more effort and time put into it. I didn't understand that if something hasn't moved after much prayer there is a legal reason for it. The devil has a legal right to withstand me. The only thing that will bring an answer is removing the legal right that the devil has to resist us. Please understand that I do believe in persevering prayer. I also have come to believe that revealed strategies will make us more effective than just praying with more force and 'doing time' in prayer. After two years of praying and seeing absolutely no results, I began to get an understanding of operating in the courts of Heaven and coming before His throne of grace.

One morning as I was seeking the Lord and spending time with Him, the Lord said, "Take Adam before My courts." I had never done anything like that before, but I was very open to try. I wasn't dealing with a national issue or a global concern. I was dealing with a personal issue, my own son. I didn't need to be before a court in Heaven that had jurisdiction over what would happen to nations. All I needed to do was be before His throne of grace and find mercy and grace for Adam in this time.

I began by simply approaching His throne of grace with boldness. We are told that because of who Jesus is and what He has done we can approach this throne with absolute confidence. Hebrews 4:14-16 tells us just some of the things that are working on our behalf before this throne of grace.

> Seeing then that we have a great High Priest who has passed through the Heavens, Jesus the Son of God, let us hold fast our confession. For we do not have a High Priest who cannot sympathize with our weaknesses, but was in all points tempted as we are, yet without sin. Let us therefore come boldly to the throne of grace, that we may obtain mercy and find grace to help in time of need (Hebrews 4:14-16).

We are told that we have a *Great High Priest* who is Jesus that is before this throne of grace on our behalf. The position of *High Priest* is a legal position before the throne. All we have to do is look at Aaron the High Priest during the Exodus adventures of the Jews to see that his job was to provide the Lord with the legal right to bless Israel. Priests give God the legal privilege to bless instead of curse a person or a thing. Aaron did this through all the sacrifices that he offered and every function of his priesthood.

This is what Jesus is doing as our High Priest now. He is before this throne of grace offering His own blood so God has a legal right to bless us instead of curse us. We don't have to be afraid to come before this throne, because of the position Jesus has won as our High Priest. Notice also that Jesus as High Priest has passed through the Heavens. This is significant. The powers of darkness that occupy these spiritual dimensions called the heavens could not stop Jesus from taking His legal place as High Priest. Because of His absolute obedience to the Father and the blood that He shed, they had no power to keep Him from His place. The result is that these principalities have now lost their legal right to rule. Jesus has legally overthrown these powers of darkness. It is our job as the Church to execute and administrate this judgment on the Earth. Colossians 2:13-15 shows us the legal position the Lord has granted us. It also clearly articulates the undoing of the previous position of the powers of darkness. We have now been granted, by the work of Jesus on the cross, a legal position in Heaven from which we can operate.

> And you, being dead in your trespasses and the uncircumcision of your flesh, He has made alive together with Him, having forgiven you all trespasses, having wiped out the handwriting of requirements that was against us, which was contrary to us. And He has taken it out of the way, having nailed it to the cross. Having disarmed principalities and powers, He made a public spectacle of them, triumphing over them in it (Colossians 2:13-15).

We must understand that the cross of Jesus was a legal transaction. We are here to execute the legalities that this transaction put into place. A legal transaction has no power if it is not executed. For instance, a judge can issue a decree of judgment in a court, but if there is no one to enforce that judgment, it will have no power. When someone is saved, it is because the legalities of what Jesus did on the cross are legally put into place in their lives. When Jesus died on the cross, He legally provided atonement for all of mankind for all ages. 2 Corinthians 5:18-19 declare to us that God in Jesus has reconciled Himself back to the world.

> Now all things are of God, who has reconciled us to Himself through Jesus Christ, and has given us the ministry of reconciliation, that is, that God was in Christ reconciling the world to Himself, not imputing their trespasses to them, and has committed to us the word of reconciliation (2 Corinthians 5:18-19).

When Jesus died on the cross, God reconciled Himself back to the world legally. Every legal issue that separated God and man was taken out of the way through the cross. Notice though that people that are saved have to 'be reconciled back to God'. They have to legally grab hold of what Jesus did and make it their own. 2 Corinthians 5:20 illustrates this.

> Now then, we are ambassadors for Christ, as though God were pleading through us: we implore you on Christ's behalf, be reconciled to God (2 Corinthians 5:20).

In response to God reconciling Himself back to us, we must be reconciled back to Him. Just because Jesus fulfilled every legal issue separating us from God doesn't mean we are automatically saved. We must legally apprehend, for ourselves, what Jesus legally provided for us. 1 John 1:9 displays this fact.

> If we confess our sins, He is faithful and just to forgive us our sins and to cleanse us from all unrighteousness (1 John 1:9).

God is faithful and just. Faithful speaks of His covenant keeping nature. He will be true to the covenant He made with us through the blood and body of Jesus. A covenant is a legal entity. This Scripture also says God is just. This means He administers justice into place. God loves justice and hates injustice. Please notice that nowhere in this Scripture is mercy mentioned. We are not forgiven and cleansed on the basis of God's mercy. We are forgiven and cleansed on the basis of His covenant keeping nature and His justice. In other words, God can legally show us mercy because a legal precedent has been set from the cross that allows the Lord from His covenant and justice to be merciful. His mercy is a result of His justice.

When we meet the legal requirements of confession, God is freed to legally forgive us of our sins. But the forgiveness released to us is found in the just nature of God. Because of what Jesus did for us on the cross, God can now legally forgive and cleanse us when we meet the legal requirement of confession. The cross of Jesus grants God the legal and just right to forgive and cleanse. We are, in essence, executing what Jesus legally purchased for us. But without our confession and repentance that legally puts forgiveness, cleansing and restoration in place, the work of Jesus is for nothing, even though He completed His job. Having a legal decree and executing it into place are two different things.

This is why repentance is so important. Our repentance grants God the legal right to display and show His mercy. Otherwise we live far below what Jesus purchased at the cross. Even though it is legally ours, we can only get it when we execute into place the verdicts of the cross.

Now, back to the story concerning my son, Adam. As Adam languished in his depressed state, the Lord told me to "take Adam to court." As I said before, I had never done this. I simply began by declaring that I intended and wanted to present Adam before God's throne of grace. As I did this, I began to repent for what Adam had allowed in his life. I repented for his lack of faith, his lying down under depression, his giving up and anything else I felt at that moment. I was endeavoring to 'silence' the accuser that was using legal things to resist Adam and his destiny. (Revelation 12:10) I will get into this in a greater dimension in a later chapter.

Just suffice it to say for the moment that the only weapon the devil has against us and our destiny in the books of Heaven is accusation. I had a right to repent on Adam's behalf as an intercessor until Adam could do it for himself and silence the accuser. This is what an 'intercessor' does. They take a legal position on behalf of another until the other can and will take it for themselves. As I repented for Adam I was getting legal things in place that had been opposing Adam. As soon as I felt that I had answered every legal thing the accuser was using against Adam, I felt a release of the Lord.

Suddenly I heard the Lord say, "Now you repent for all the negative things you have said about Adam in your frustration." I realized at that moment that when I had spoken negative things about Adam, I had actually empowered the accuser against Him. When I had said, "I don't understand why he won't stand up and fight", or "Why won't he get up and move forward?", I had inadvertently empowered the accuser with my 'testimony' concerning Adam. The Lord showed me that the accuser before the throne was actually saying, "Even his own father says these things about him." When people in authority over us speak against us or for us, it becomes testimony before Heaven. Jesus said in Matthew 12:36-37 that our words set legal things in place.

> But I say to you that for every idle word men may speak, they will give account of it in the day of judgment. For by your words you will be justified, and by your words you will be condemned" (Matthew 12:36-37).

The word *idle* actually means something *unemployed*. In other words, we don't mean it, but we say it anyway. These words become testimony before the courts of Heaven that can justify or condemn.

I was being used of the devil to empower his accusations against Adam in the court of Heaven. I then repented of that which I had spoken against Adam from my place of frustration. I immediately felt a release come as legalities began to be put into place in Heaven concerning Adam. I was answering the accusation in the court of Heaven that was legally being used to hold Adam captive in depression. Everything is a legal matter when it comes to Heaven and the spirit realm. We must learn to get things legally in place before we march onto any battlefield.

As soon as I had repented for both Adam and myself, I then began to '*prophesy*' and '*decree*' what was written in Adam's book in Heaven. Remember that each one of us has a book in Heaven with our destinies and days written in it (Psalm 139:15-16). As I had removed everything that was working against Adam legally, I now could prophesy from his book what God had said about him. I began to prophesy the portions of his destiny that I felt were in his book. I broke the spirit of depression and told it to leave. I immediately felt things shift.

A week and a half later, I received a call from Adam. This is what he said. "Dad, I don't know what happened. But a week and a half ago all the depression suddenly was gone. I am free from it and am ready to pursue what God made me for." What I had not been able to accomplish in two years of praying, warring, yelling, crying and every other emotional appeal before God, was done in about a fifteen minute period of being before the throne of grace and getting legal things in place.

Adam is back in full-time ministry as an associate pastor in the Northwest part of our nation. Once legal things were dealt with in the courts of Heaven, the power of depression was broken. The Father's heart was free to come into operation over Adam. He is presently living out his dream of ministry and the dream that God has for him. He is apprehending what is in his book that is written in Heaven.

There is a very real court of Heaven that we have been granted entrance into. From this court we are to get legal things in place so destinies written in the book of Heaven can be fulfilled. In the next chapter I will show us some more of the things I have learned about this process.

4

Books and Destinies

Everything in the spirit realm is about legalities. God has given mankind freedom of choice and therefore He can do nothing unless we give him the legal right. The devil, also, can do nothing unless it is legally allowed. We, as people of the Earth, grant the legal permission for either the devil to work or God to work. Matthew 16:18-19 tells us that we as the Church or Ecclesia of God have been given the right to bind and loose.

> And I also say to you that you are Peter, and on this rock I will build My church, and the gates of Hades shall not prevail against it. And I will give you the keys of the kingdom of Heaven, and whatever you bind on earth will be bound in Heaven, and whatever you loose on earth will be loosed in Heaven" (Matthew 16:18-19).

The word *Ecclesia* is the word translated church from the Greek. This word means the judicial, legislative and governmental people of God. It speaks of a people that have been granted legal positions on Earth and before the Lord. We have been given the right and authority to get things legally in place so that God's will can come into the Earth realm.

The words bind and loose are actually legal terms at their root. The word bind speaks of getting a binding contract into place, while the word loose speaks of dissolving an existing contract. Jesus was saying that the Ecclesia has a judicial responsibility to establish binding contracts with Heaven that allow God the legal right to invade and impact the planet. The Ecclesia also has the job of legally dissolving contracts with the devil that allow him to operate in the Earth. When we learn to get legal things in place, we can then see the devil expelled and God's will established. This is our job individually and corporately.

Answering the Accuser

This happened in Peter's life. Jesus went into the courts of Heaven on behalf of Peter and secured the destiny written in the books of Heaven for him. Luke 22:31-32 tell us that Satan desired to have Peter.

> And the Lord said, "Simon, Simon! Indeed, Satan has asked for you, that he may sift you as wheat. But I have prayed for you, that your faith should not fail; and when you have returned to Me, strengthen your brethren" (Luke 22:31-32).

The words **asked for** in the Greek actually says **demanded for trial**. Satan came and demanded that Peter be put on trial in the courts of Heaven. Satan had developed evidence against Peter to try and thwart what was written in the books of Heaven about him. Remember that when the court is seated, the books are opened (Daniel 7:10). The devil understood something of what was in Peter's book. He understood the significant purpose Peter was to play in the Kingdom of God. He knew that Peter was destined by Heaven to have a radical and dramatic effect.

If the devil didn't stop him, Peter would do massive damage to his empire and establish the Kingdom of God. Satan, therefore, had to have a scheme to stop Peter if he could. His plan was to bring him to court and put him on trial. The reason for this was to disqualify Peter legally from what was written in his book. If Satan could disqualify Peter through accusation in court, he could stop the agenda of God for the Earth.

We must realize that Satan is an accuser. Revelation 12:10-11 shows that Satan is accusing us day and night.

> Then I heard a loud voice saying in Heaven, "Now salvation, and strength, and the kingdom of our God, and the power of His Christ have come, for the accuser of our brethren, who accused them before our God day and night, has been cast down. And they overcame him by the blood of the Lamb and by the word of their testimony, and they did not love their lives to the death (Revelation 12:10-11).

Satan is before the throne of God seeking to present evidence in the courts as to why we are disqualified from what is in our books. He wants to stop us, at any cost, from stepping into the destinies written about us in our books. It is our job to answer these accusations and silence them so that God has the legal right to grant us what is written in our books. When this occurs we fulfill our life's destiny and God's Kingdom purposes are done.

The only way the devil can stop us from fulfilling what is in the books, is through accusation. This was the tactic he used against Peter. It is the tactic that he used against Job. Job 1:6-12 shows us activity in the courts of Heaven.

> Now there was a day when the sons of God came to present themselves before the Lord, and Satan also came among them. And the Lord said to Satan, "From where do you come?" So Satan answered the Lord and said, "From going to and fro on the Earth, and from walking back and forth on it."
>
> Then the Lord said to Satan, "Have you considered My servant Job, that there is none like him on the Earth, a blameless and upright man, one who fears God and shuns evil?"
>
> So Satan answered the Lord and said, "Does Job fear God for nothing? Have You not made a hedge around him, around his household, and around all that he has on every side? You have blessed the work of his hands, and his possessions have increased in the land. But now, stretch out Your hand and touch all that he has, and he will surely curse You to Your face!"
>
> And the Lord said to Satan, "Behold, all that he has is in your power; only do not lay a hand on his person." So Satan went out from the presence of the Lord (Job 1:6-12).

Satan brings accusations against Job. He accuses Job of serving God with impure motives. As a result of this accusation, Job is thrown into devastation. The Lord as judge allows the devil to operate against Job. I don't have all the answers as to why this was allowed by God, but clearly the devil brought enough accusations against Job that God legally allowed the persecution to occur. Perhaps, there was no one to answer the accusations brought against Job. This was prior to the cross of Jesus and there was not yet an intercessor or one to stand on Job's behalf.

Regardless, it is clear that the tribulation of Job was a result of the accusation of Satan.

It is interesting that the accusation that Satan brought against Job was concerning his motives for serving God. It wasn't about a personal sin or a sin in his lineage or family line. The accusation was that Job only served God because God had a hedge about him and he couldn't be touched. Satan's lambasting of Job was that if life wasn't so good, Job wouldn't serve God. Wow! The accusation was concerning impure motives. In other words, we must not just do the right things; we must do the right things for the right reasons. This is why we must consistently allow the Lord to judge the motives and intents of our hearts. We must cry out with the Psalmist, "*Search me O God and see if their be any wicked ways in me*". (Psalm 139:23-24) When we do, we take away from the devil any potential realms of accusation he could use against us.

What we must also realize is Job was rewarded in the end with a double portion. Job 42:10 shows that God in His justice restored Job's fortunes.

> And the Lord restored Job's losses when he prayed for his friends. Indeed the Lord gave Job twice as much as he had before (Job 42:10).

Restoration is always a result of legal activity in the courts of Heaven. God decreed a double portion restoration for all Job had suffered. Job had to first pray for the friends who had accused him during his troubles rather than stand with him. It is interesting that when Job prayed for his friends, it granted the courts of Heaven the legal right to restore his fortunes. How often are we not getting our restoration because we will not forgive and release? When Job followed through with prayer and forgiveness, the court rendered verdicts in his behalf of restitution and restoration of all that had been lost. Job qualified himself for this through his faithfulness toward God. The judicial system of Heaven ruled in his favor.

Standing in Holiness

Joshua the High Priest in Zechariah 3:1-7 is being accused of uncleanness and resisted by Satan.

> Then he showed me Joshua the high priest standing before the Angel of the Lord, and Satan standing at his right hand to oppose him. And the Lord said to Satan, "The Lord rebuke you, Satan! The Lord who has chosen Jerusalem rebuke you! Is this not a brand plucked from the fire?"
>
> Now Joshua was clothed with filthy garments, and was standing before the Angel.
>
> Then He answered and spoke to those who stood before Him, saying, "Take away the filthy garments from him." And to him He said, "See, I have removed your iniquity from you, and I will clothe you with rich robes."
>
> And I said, "Let them put a clean turban on his head."
>
> So they put a clean turban on his head, and they put the clothes on him. And the Angel of the Lord stood by.
>
> Then the Angel of the Lord admonished Joshua, saying, "Thus says the Lord of hosts:
> 'If you will walk in My ways,
> And if you will keep My command, Then you shall

also judge My house, And likewise have charge of
My courts; I will give you places to walk
Among these who stand here (Zechariah 3:1-7).

Satan comes to resist and accuse Joshua of uncleanness. He is
resisting him because of what God needed to do through him.
The purpose of God through Joshua the High Priest was to
rebuild and re-establish Jerusalem. The devil's tactic to stop
this from happening was to bring accusation against the one
that God would do it through. Our cleanness and holiness is
essential to God's will being done. Without it, Satan can stop
what God will do through us with accusations.

The Lord's answer to the uncleanness of Joshua was to
rebuke Satan. Notice He didn't rebuke Satan for Joshua's
sake. He rebuked Satan for the sake of Jerusalem being rebuilt.
Sometimes our greatest asset is what God has called us to do.
Once Satan was rebuked, Joshua needed to be cleaned up or
Satan would have come back and legally resisted him again.
Joshua's uncleanness granted Satan the legal right to resist him
and what God was doing through him. The result was that the
angels began to clean him up. Then the prophet began to cleanse
him as well. Notice that the angels are putting clean garments on
Joshua in this spiritual atmosphere. But Zechariah the prophet
then proclaims a clean turban on his head. In order to be free
from any place the devil can accuse us, we need angelic and
prophetic input. With these things working on Joshua's behalf,
he was cleansed.

Notice the result. If he would stay clean and walk righteously,
he would be granted charge of the courts of the Lord and he
would judge the house of the Lord. In other words, he would
be given authority in the courts of Heaven to be able to render
judgments that set things in order. If we are to operate in the

judicial place God has for us, we must be cleansed and purified for that operation. We are then granted authority because we have overcome the accusations of the devil and can access what is written in our book.

Before we move into what happened with Peter, we need to understand the way the devil accuses us. Before Satan was cast out of Heaven, he was a part of the judicial operation. Ezekiel 28:14 says that Satan, when he was Lucifer in Heaven, walked on the fiery stones. This is a reference to the courts of the Lord and His Throne.

> "You were the anointed cherub who covers;
> I established you; You were on the holy mountain of
> God; You walked back and forth in the midst of fiery
> stones (Ezekiel 28:14).

This was before his fall. He was a part of the legal system of Heaven. One of his jobs was to gather evidence through his walking so God could render verdicts based on it. We then see him after his being cast out still walking. Job 1:7 shows that, as Satan, he was still walking.

> And the Lord said to Satan, "From where do you
> come?"
> So Satan answered the Lord and said, "From going
> to and fro on the earth, and from walking back and
> forth on it" (Job 1:7).

Now Satan is walking about on the Earth during Job's days. But when we get to 1 Peter 5:8 we see why he is walking.

> Be sober, be vigilant; because your adversary the devil walks about like a roaring lion, seeking whom he may devour (1 Peter 5:8).

Satan is walking about to seek whom he may devour. Remember, Satan can only devour when he has a legal reason. His walking about is for the purpose of gathering evidence so he can accuse and be granted legal rights to destroy. This could explain why we see bad things happen to good people. Somewhere in their lives or history and ancestry the devil finds a legal right to bring destruction. The devil can do nothing unless he finds a legal place he can exploit through his walking about.

When Satan comes before the Throne of God regarding Job, the Lord asked him where he had been. His response was, "From going to and fro on the Earth and walking back and forth on it". The Lord then says to Satan, "Have you considered my servant Job?" in other words, "Have you gathered any evidence against Him"? This is when Satan brings up the whole motive issue. The Lord knew that Satan's walking back and forth was a searching out of people who had Kingdom destinies.

This is exactly what he had done with Peter. He targeted Peter because of the tremendous things in his book. He had gathered evidence against Peter to disqualify him from what was in his book. He had presented it to Heaven and demanded a court date concerning Peter. But Jesus said, "I have prayed for you." Through the prayers of Jesus, Peter was not disqualified, he was qualified for his destiny. I want to look at what happened in the courts of Heaven that allowed Peter to be secured for his future and fulfill what was in the books of Heaven about him.

The Power and Authority Granted Us in the Courts of Heaven

The first thing that allowed Peter's destiny to be secured was Jesus' prayers. Luke 22:31-32 shows that Satan demanded Peter be put on trial, but Jesus stood for him in the courts of Heaven.

> And the Lord said, "Simon, Simon! Indeed, Satan has asked for you, that he may sift you as wheat. But I have prayed for you, that your faith should not fail; and when you have returned to Me, strengthen your brethren" (Luke 22:31-32).

Everyone would probably think, "Well of course it worked, Jesus prayed for him." What we must realize is that this was BEFORE Jesus died, was buried, resurrected and ascended. In other words this was before He won His position in the courts of Heaven. What Jesus did for Peter, he did as a mortal man. This is important otherwise we disqualify ourselves from what we have been called to do. When Jesus prayed for Peter, he didn't do it as God. He did it as a mortal man.

Philippians 2:5-11 shows us that Jesus lived on Earth as a mortal man. He never once touched His God-powers while here. Everything He did, he did as a man filled with God, not as God.

> Let this mind be in you which was also in Christ Jesus, who, being in the form of God, did not consider it robbery to be equal with God, but made Himself of no reputation, taking the form of a bondservant, and coming in the likeness of men. And being found

in appearance as a man, He humbled Himself and became obedient to the point of death, even the death of the cross. Therefore God also has highly exalted Him and given Him the name which is above every name, that at the name of Jesus every knee should bow, of those in Heaven, and of those on Earth, and of those under the Earth, and that every tongue should confess that Jesus Christ is Lord, to the glory of God the Father (Philippians 2:5-11).

We are told in these Scriptures that Jesus laid aside all of His God-powers and functioned here totally as a human being. Because of His obedience to the Father to do this, He won for Himself a Name greater than all other names. This speaks of the position Jesus holds in Heaven. If Jesus had touched His God-powers while living on the Earth, He would have forfeited the right to be our Savior. Adam, a human being, lost creation. Jesus, the second and last Adam, had to live totally as a human being to win it back.

This is why Satan tempted Jesus in the wilderness with, "If you are the Son of God, turn these stones into bread" (Matthew 4: 3). Satan knew that if Jesus ever touched His God-powers while living on the Earth, He would lose the right to redeem it back to God. The temptation was to use His powers as God to turn the stones into bread.

How did Jesus do what He did while on Earth, if He didn't touch His God-powers? He lived not as God on the planet but rather as a man filled with God. This is what happened at the river Jordan when the Holy Spirit descended on Him. This is why the term *Incarnate One* is used to describe Jesus. Incarnate means a *body filled with a spirit*. This is the way Jesus lived. He never did one recorded miracle until the Holy Spirit filled Him.

He lived the exact same way that we are to live. Not as God, but as people filled with God. This means everything He did is legal for us to do as well. If Jesus had performed miracles as God, then we would be excluded from such activity. We are not God, but part of humanity.

This is important concerning Jesus' prayer for Peter. He did not intercede in the courts of Heaven as High Priest or even as God. He had not yet won that position. His prayer for Peter was as a man filled with God and under the unction of the Holy Spirit.

In other words what He did for Peter we can also do. Just like Jesus went into the courts of Heaven and secured Peter's destiny, we too can go into the courts of Heaven and secure our destinies that are in the books. We can secure the destinies of others that are joined to us as well. The main thing is that we should not disqualify ourselves from the power and authority we have in Heaven and its court system.

Closing Doors Opened Through Sin

Another necessary thing that must be done to secure our futures from the books is to realize that Satan will exploit anything possible. Most of us have enough personal issues that supply the devil with accusations to last a lifetime. As big of an issue as this is, there can be an even larger one. We must realize that anything in our bloodline can be legal fodder with which Satan can accuse us. In other words, if people in our bloodline have sexual sins, perversions, covenant breaking, innocent bloodshed, thievery, allegiance to other gods and idols, demonic worship and other things, the devil can exploit this in the courts of Heaven to resist what is written in the books about us. I am not talking about deliverance from personal demons. I am referring to sins in the bloodline from perhaps centuries or millenniums before, where someone opened a legal door that Satan can use to stop destinies. This is seen in Isaiah, chapter 43:25-28.

> "I, even I, am He who blots out your transgressions for My own sake;
> And I will not remember your sins. Put Me in remembrance;
> Let us contend together;
> State your case, that you may be acquitted. Your first father sinned,
> And your mediators have transgressed against Me.
> Therefore I will profane the princes of the sanctuary;
> I will give Jacob to the curse,
> And Israel to reproaches (Isaiah 43:25-28).

There are several issues in this Scripture. Notice that God is speaking from a courtroom perspective. When He says, "State your case and be acquitted," this is the language of court settings. The word acquitted actually means to be justified. All the accusations against us have been silenced and God is free to deliver to us our destinies. Also notice that in this scenario, the destiny of a nation hangs in the balance. God is saying that because there is improper activity or inadequate operations in the court of Heaven, Jacob is given over to a curse and Israel to reproaches. Operation in the courts of Heaven can be on a personal level but it can go all the way up to the destinies of nations being fulfilled. In this Scripture the reason a nation was being afflicted was because of the first father's sin. It goes on to say that the transgressions of a mediator can also prohibit the destiny of a nation from being realized. Before I go into these two things, I need to point out some other realities concerning operations in the courts of Heaven.

The Lord says that He blots out our transgressions for His own sake. This means that God needs us. The saving of nations is not a sovereign act. The Lord needs our co-operation in the courts of Heaven. We need to accept His forgiveness and walk in it. I usually tell people, "For God's sake, forgive yourself." He needs us to embrace the grace of His forgiveness so we can stand in the courts and work with Him to get his will done in nations.

Then the Lord says, "Put Me in remembrance." Remember we are in court. When He says, "Put Me in remembrance," He is saying that we should remind Him of what He wrote in the books of Heaven. Call God into remembrance concerning what He said about you or a church or a business or a family or even a nation. God is saying, "Give Me a legal reason to fulfill what I previously ordained." This is our job. We are to grant God the legal reason to show mercy and fulfill what is written in the books of Heaven. Then the Lord says, "Let us contend together." Remember that this is from a courtroom setting. This Scripture does not mean that we should contend with **Him**, but rather that we are going to contend **with Him** against the accuser. Together we will answer every accusation until God legally can grant what was written in the books. God is not our enemy. We are together with Him as individuals and also as the Ecclesia granting God the legal right to fulfill His passions. Once this is in place the Kingdom rule of God legally comes into Earth spheres.

The Transgressions of the Mediators

Notice that there are two things that can hinder us from getting verdicts for nations and ourselves. They are the mediator's transgressions and first fathers' sins. The word mediator in the Hebrew means one who is attempting to speak a foreign language. A court system has its own language. If you are not educated in speaking the language of the court you will not be effective. Attorneys go to school for many years learning the law and how to speak the language of the courts. They learn the protocol of the judicial system so they can be heard. Without a proper knowledge of this system and an adherence to it they cannot function nor gain verdicts from the courts. Neither can we in the courts of Heaven. Proper behavior and protocol is necessary if we are to be effective in this ultimate court system.

God said through Isaiah that these mediators (which is a legal term and function) had sinned. In other words their sin had caused them to lose their place and authority in the courts of Heaven. We may be able to bluff our way through things on Earth, but if there is sin in our lives, the spirit realm knows it. When we have not dealt with sin in our lives, we forfeit any and all authority in the courts of Heaven. In Isaiah 43, the result was a nation coming under curses, reproaches and judgment. Could it be that the reason we have not been effective in turning nations to their Kingdom purpose is because those of us who were to have authority in Heaven have forfeited it because of our sin? May we repent, and the Lord forgive us. Nations hang in the balance. We must learn to operate in the courts of Heaven and grant the Lord His legal right to bless the nations and us again. It is His heart to bless us, but we must grant Him the legal right to do so.

The First Fathers' Sins

The other issue that was causing nations to fall short of the destiny written in the books concerning them, was the first fathers' sin. This speaks of not my personal sin, but the sin connected to my bloodline. If there are sins that have contaminated my bloodline from even thousands of years gone by, this grants the accuser the legal right to resist me in the courts of Heaven. This is why we see Nehemiah, Daniel and others repenting for the sins of their forefathers. They understood that until these sins that had allowed the devil to bring them into captivity were dealt with legally, there would be no deliverance. The devil would have a legal reason to afflict and hold them until that legal reason was taken away. Nehemiah, for instance, repented for himself, his nation and its history so that in the courts of Heaven the accuser would be silenced. We see this in Nehemiah 1:5-7.

> And I said: "I pray, Lord God of Heaven, O great and awesome God, You who keep Your covenant and mercy with those who love You and observe Your commandments, please let Your ear be attentive and Your eyes open, that You may hear the prayer of Your servant which I pray before You now, day and night, for the children of Israel Your servants, and confess the sins of the children of Israel which we have sinned against You. Both my father's house and I have sinned. We have acted very corruptly against You, and have not kept the commandments, the statutes, nor the ordinances which You commanded Your servant Moses (Nehemiah 1:5-7).

Nehemiah repented for himself, his nation, his fathers' sins and his history that granted the devil legal rights to afflict him. This is a picture of the first fathers' sin. If the devil cannot find a legal reason in my own personal life to stop what is in the books about me, he will search my bloodline. We see him doing this with Jesus. John 14:30 shows that the devil came and searched Jesus out, but found no place to accuse Him.

> I will no longer talk much with you, for the ruler
> of this world is coming, and he has nothing in Me
> (John 14:30).

The reason the devil could find nothing in Jesus was because He lived a perfect life but also had a perfect bloodline. His bloodline was from God the Father through the Holy Spirit. Our bloodline though is not perfect. There are all sorts of things the devil can unveil as he searches us out. When he finds something that is not dealt with in our bloodline, it gives him a legal right to resist us with that thing. The truth is that the devil will not bother with our bloodline until we become a governmental threat against him. We see this same strategy in the political arena all the time. When someone begins to rise on the political scene during election periods they always become a target. Their attempt to take a high governmental position causes their adversaries to search them out and their history. They are seeking to find a place of accusation that will damage them and disqualify them from the office they seek. This is very similar to what happens in the spirit realm when we begin to step into governmental places of authority to shift things.

The more we become ones that can step into the courts of Heaven and get things legally in place, the more he will seek a way to stop us. Remember, his only weapon against us is accusation in the courts. Every other attack flows from accusations made.

I personally experienced this. I was privileged to develop and lead an apostolic center that was a strong display of God's grace in the Earth. We had the supernatural flowing, healing occurring, prosperity in place and we were impacting the region for the Kingdom. The Lord then spoke to my wife, Mary, and I to hand this ministry off and begin to launch into a bigger Kingdom sphere. We obeyed and did what we were told to do. What I didn't understand was that when I transitioned from a local sphere of ministry to a national and even international one, I became a bigger threat to the devil. I had no known sin in my life. I sought to live a holy lifestyle before the Lord. We had blessings in every dimension in our home and family. Life was good. When we stepped out of the local ministry and into a bigger Kingdom effect, everything changed. One of the main things that occurred was that literally millions of dollars were stolen from us. I had very diligently sought to have things properly ordered so that we would have plenty of finances to do the ministry God had assigned to us. As I was no longer leading a local work, I had spent years getting things financially in place so Mary and I could do whatever we were called to do. I was sure everything was properly ordered. What I didn't understand was legal fight I was engaging.

I don't want to bore you with details. Just suffice it to say that people whom I trusted implicitly turned against me and incited others to do the same. This resulted in personal and financial devastation. We went from a very secure future to having to wonder how we could pay the bills from month to month, week to week and even day to day. Even though the Lord was faithful, I still wondered how this had happened. We had faithfully obeyed in every area and had always practiced the principles of honor. We had obeyed the Lord in all forms of giving. We had shown mercy to people many times. We had always taken care of our leaders and others as well. Now it seemed that everything we had done to secure our future hadn't worked. I really wondered why this had happened as I sought to navigate through those very difficult days.

Then I began to learn about bloodlines and the courts of Heaven. As I was preparing to minister for a particular group, the leader said they would like to cleanse my bloodline. This group is highly apostolic and prophetic. I agreed for this to be done. As we began to go into the courts of the Lord one of the seer prophets suddenly said that someone in my bloodline and history had made a covenant with a demonic god named Parax. Someone pulled out the computer and Googled Parax. To my astonishment there was a demonic god named Parax and its chief characteristic was to 'suck dry'. Instantly a light came on for me. I realized that as I became a bigger threat in the spirit realm, the devil and his forces had searched out my bloodline and found that an ancestor connected to me had made a covenant with this demonic entity. This gave the devil the legal right to go after all that Mary and I had built and steal it away. I knew that what we had experienced was not a result of our own personal sin, but the result of a sin in my bloodline that granted the devil a legal right to resist and attack me. Finally, I understood what had stood against me. I repented for the ones in my ancestry that had made this covenant and then renounced and broke that covenant off my family line. The result was that a new realm of blessing began to break through in my life.

The devil will search our bloodlines and find ways to accuse us legally. We must know how to cleanse our bloodlines consistently so that we can take up our authority in the courts of Heaven without fear of backlash.

This is why before every restoration that occurred in Bible times, there was not just repentance for personal sin, but also for "Fathers' sins." For instance when Nehemiah began to cry out for the restoration of Israel and especially Jerusalem, he repented for his own sins and the sins of his fathers. Nehemiah 1:4-6 show the prayers that Nehemiah prayed to begin the restoration process.

> So it was, when I heard these words, that I sat down and wept, and mourned for many days; I was fasting and praying before the God of heaven. And I said: "I pray, LORD God of heaven, O great and awesome God, You who keep Your covenant and mercy with those who love You and observe Your commandments, please let Your ear be attentive and Your eyes open, that You may hear the prayer of Your servant which I pray before You now, day and night, for the children of Israel Your servants, and confess the sins of the children of Israel which we have sinned against You. Both my father's house and I have sinned (Nehemiah 1:4-6).

When Nehemiah repented for his fathers' sin, he was not endeavoring to alter their eternal state. Their own life had established what that status would be. The purpose of his repentance was to snatch from the devil the legal right to keep Israel in a place of captivity and oppression. It was the "fathers' sins" that had legally allowed this to occur. To get Israel free and Jerusalem restored, something legal had to shift in the spirit realm. Someone had to ask for and receive mercy from the Lord. Once the mercy of God against their sin was received, legal issues in the heavenly realm were altered. God could now have a legal right to undo the captivity of the Jews and bring restoration to them and their land. But without dealing with the "fathers' sins" that had allowed it, nothing would be able to shift. Sin does not just disappear over time. It only disappears when someone grabs hold of the blood of Jesus and appropriates it into place against that sin. When this is done, legal things come into order and heaven moves as a result.

This is what was happening with Peter. My suspicion is that Peter had plenty of personal issues the devil could use against him, but I am sure that the devil had searched Peter's bloodline and had found reasons to accuse him before Heaven. Jesus went into that trial setting, interceded for Peter and answered those accusations. The result was that Peter did step into his destiny. The devil was not successful in causing Peter to be disqualified. Peter shook the Earth and nations and fulfilled what was written in his book.

We will, too, when we learn to operate in the courts of Heaven and answer the accusations of the enemy. Not only do our individual destinies hang in the balance, but the destinies of nations as well. Let's grant God the legal right to fulfill the passion of His heart and what He wrote in the books before time began.

5

Voices in the Courts

There are many different voices in a court. There is the voice of the judge, the voice of the attorneys, the voice of witnesses, the voice of bailiffs, the voice of recorders, the voice of the jury and others as well. There are also many different voices in the courts of Heaven. Our job is to understand these voices and come into agreement with them. As we join with these voices and release our faith and agreement with them, God's Kingdom will on Earth is then free to be accomplished.

Any lack of the Kingdom being manifest is because of a legal issue. The Father's heart is very clear. God is not withholding from us. If there is a lack of manifestation of Kingdom purpose, it is because we have yet to grant the Father the legal right to fulfill His passion toward us. If we are praying according to the will of God and have prayed for an extended time without results, something legal is standing in the way of the answer. Somewhere in the spirit realm the demonic powers have found a legal right to resist the answer from coming to us. The accuser of the brethren is speaking against us. The answer to this is to learn and agree with the voices in the court of Heaven. When we do, the accuser is silenced and we set in motion Heaven to be manifest in the Earth.

You Have Come to Mount Zion

In order to understand the different voices operating in the courts of Heaven we have to understand 'Zion'. Hebrews 12:22-24 tells us where we have been positioned as New Testament believers.

> But you have come to Mount Zion and to the city of the living God, the Heavenly Jerusalem, to an innumerable company of angels, to the general assembly and church of the firstborn who are registered in Heaven, to God the Judge of all, to the spirits of just men made perfect, to Jesus the Mediator of the new covenant, and to the blood of sprinkling that speaks better things than that of Abel (Hebrews 12:22-24).

In the preceding verses we are told that we haven't come to Mount Sinai, which was the place where the Law was given. We have not come to the place of legalism and of death. In that place the children of Israel were afraid to approach God and did not even want to hear His voice. This place was necessary in that it was where the Law was given. The Law served to bring us to Christ, but it was not to be the place where we stayed. It was to be a part of the journey, but not the destination. The destination was to be Mount Zion. The earthly manifestation of Mount Zion was established by King David as a place where perpetual worship was offered. It is where David set up the ark of the covenant and had 24-hour worship every day. This was one of the first orders of business that David performed once he became king of all of Israel.

People think that Zion is therefore about worship. But Zion

is not about worship. It is about the purpose of worship. King David commissioned worship to cultivate and host the presence of the Lord so that from that presence, he could govern a nation. This is the purpose of worship. Out of worship is to flow the governing authority of God through His church. When we worship there is to be a rearranging of the heavenly or spiritual realm until Heaven is allowed to enter Earth. This is what Psalm 110:1-2 declares.

> The Lord said to my Lord, "Sit at My right hand,
> Till I make Your enemies Your footstool."
> The Lord shall send the rod of Your strength out of
> Zion. Rule in the midst of Your enemies!
> (Psalm 110:1-2)

Notice what is declared about Zion. The rod of the strength of the Lord will flow out of Zion and cause the enemies of God to be subdued. The purpose of the activity of Zion is rulership and governmental authority. The activity of Zion is worship that allows the Lord's rod of strength to be wielded against His enemies.

When the Word of the Lord says that we have come to Zion, it is saying we have come to this governmental place in God. We have been privileged out of a place of intimate worship with the Lord to govern with Him. We are no longer at Mount Sinai but now at Mount Zion, the place of His governing power.

Also, please be aware, that we are not trying to get to Zion. We have been granted as New Testament believers to be there already. One of the problems with us as the Church, is that we are still trying to get to a place that we have already been positioned in. If we could simply understand the divine placement of the Lord in our life, we would begin to function in faith and see things we have been waiting on begin to happen. Yet so often we are striving to get positioned when we have already been positioned by the Lord and His grace. If we can by revelation understand this and begin to function from that place, we will begin to exercise Kingdom rule. *We have come to Mount Zion.*

The Mountain of the Lord's House

To further understand what we have come to, we should consider Isaiah 2:1-4.

> The word that Isaiah the son of Amoz saw concerning
> Judah and Jerusalem.
> Now it shall come to pass in the latter days
> That the mountain of the Lord's house
> Shall be established on the top of the mountains,
> And shall be exalted above the hills;
> And all nations shall flow to it.
> Many people shall come and say,
> "Come, and let us go up to the mountain of the Lord,
> To the house of the God of Jacob;
> He will teach us His ways,
> And we shall walk in His paths."
> For out of Zion shall go forth the law,
> And the word of the Lord from Jerusalem.
> He shall judge between the nations,
> And rebuke many people;
> They shall beat their swords into plowshares,
> And their spears into pruning hooks;
> Nation shall not lift up sword against nation,
> Neither shall they learn war anymore (Isaiah 2:1-4).

We see that the mountain of the Lord's House will be established in the top of the mountains. The word top is the Hebrew word *rosh* and it means *head*. It is saying that the mountain of the Lord's house will be the *head* of all other mountains. Anytime we read about mountains in Scripture they are speaking of governments, seen and unseen.

We see this in Jesus speaking with His disciples after their unsuccessful attempt to cast the demon out of the boy. This story is found in Matthew 17:19-21. Jesus informs them that if they have faith as a grain of mustard seed, they can speak to *this mountain* and it would move. Jesus was informing them that one of the reasons why they could not help the boy was because they were dealing with a *demonic mountain* in the spirit. This was no ordinary demonic situation. For whatever reason, this boy had become a place of a demonic government. The power and authority required to deal with this was greater than a normal circumstance. Because they hadn't recognized this, they had been unsuccessful. There are times when we encounter not just demonic imps that need to be cast out, but demonic mountains that have become governmental in nature and function. This requires a greater realm of authority to move them out of the way.

When it says the mountain of the Lord's house is in the top of the mountains, it is saying that the government of God will rule over all other governments. This reference to the mountain of the Lord's house is very interesting. The best way I know how to relate what I believe the Lord is saying here is through a dream that a prophet's wife had about me. In her dream her husband, the prophet, and I had identical garages standing next to each other. The moment I heard there were garages in the dream, I knew it spoke of a ministry center. Garages house vehicles. Vehicles almost always speak of ministry, business and anything that is being led or directed. When I dream about driving a car, flying a plane or anything like that, I know God is speaking about the ministry I direct and lead. When she told me about the garages, I knew it spoke of that which housed the ministry.

She went on to relay that as she entered her husband's garage it looked like a normal garage. But as she entered my garage, it had a mountain in it although you couldn't tell it from the outside. When she told me the dream, I wondered if there was a mountain in my garage because I lived in Colorado. I didn't yet understand that mountains spoke of government. As I became aware of this concept I knew that God was saying that He was raising a ministry center that would have a mountain in it. He was raising a House with a Mountain in it. It would look like a normal house from the outside, but it would be a governmental people that would exercise governmental authority from the mountain in the house.

This is what God is doing today. He is causing to arise Houses with Mountains in them. They may look like normal churches from the outside, but they are governmental on the inside. They are not interested in just having good activities and service and being blessed. They want to see the Kingdom of God come to the Earth. They want to see life reflect a Kingdom culture in the planet. They are houses with mountains in them. We see this same concept echoed in Isaiah 56:7.

> Even them I will bring to My holy mountain, And make them joyful in My house of prayer. Their burnt offerings and their sacrifices Will be accepted on My altar;
> For My house shall be called a house of prayer for all nations" (Isaiah 56:7).

Notice the words *house* and *mountain* are used interchangeably here. God brings these people to the holy mountain and makes them joyful in the house of prayer. So the house is in the mountain and the mountain is in the house. God's intention has always been to have a house that had a mountain in it. His desire is a house that is governmental and has influence and authority over all other forms of government in the spirit realm. From this mountain of the Lord's house the other mountains begin to reflect a Kingdom culture. This is an Old Testament picture of what Jesus said He would build in Matthew 16:18-19.

> And I also say to you that you are Peter, and on this rock I will build My church, and the gates of Hades shall not prevail against it. And I will give you the keys of the kingdom of Heaven, and whatever you bind on earth will be bound in Heaven, and whatever you loose on earth will be loosed in Heaven" (Matthew 16:18-19).

The Church that Jesus said He would build is from the Greek word Ecclesia. An *Ecclesia* within the Greek and Roman culture of Jesus' day spoke of a governmental, legislative and judicial body that made decisions and judgments that determined how society functioned. When Jesus said He would build this kind of people, He was speaking of building a house with a mountain in it. It is very important that we understand this.

This means that as the Ecclesia of God we have been given the right to stand in the courts of Heaven, which are found inside the mountain of the Lord's House. From there we are to exercise our authority as the Ecclesia that will allow what is in the books of Heaven to come to Earth. As we take up our place in the courts of Heaven inside the mountain, we become a part of God's government in the Earth. This is the place we have been given as those who have 'Come to Mount Zion'.

To further understand this, let's go back to Isaiah 2. In these verses we see that the mountain of the Lord's house is in the top of the mountains. As we continue to read about this house with a mountain in it, we discover that God actually identifies this mountain and it has a name. Isaiah chapter 2:3 tells us this mountain's name.

> Many people shall come and say,
> "Come, and let us go up to the mountain of the Lord,
> To the house of the God of Jacob;
> He will teach us His ways,
> And we shall walk in His paths."
> For out of Zion shall go forth the law,
> And the word of the Lord from Jerusalem
> (Isaiah 2:3).

This verse says that people will come and inspire each other to go up to this mountain/house. They then identify the mountains name. They say it is Zion. From Mount Zion the law will go forth. When Hebrews 12: 22 says we have come to Mount Zion, it is saying we have arrived at the governmental and judicial authority of the Lord and have become the house with a mountain in it. When we come to Mount Zion, we are commissioned and authorized to operate in the court system of Heaven. From this position we can begin to read what is written in the books of Heaven and legally administrate them into the Earth. The Word, through our function of faith, will become flesh in the Earth.

Discipling Nations from Mount Zion

Notice also in Isaiah 2:4 that through the operation in the mountain of the Lord's house, nations are judged and set in order.

> He shall judge between the nations,
> And rebuke many people;
> They shall beat their swords into plowshares,
> And their spears into pruning hooks;
> Nation shall not lift up sword against nation,
> Neither shall they learn war anymore
> (Isaiah 2:4).

From the mountain of the Lord's house He (Jesus) will judge nations. Jesus will judge nations from the house with the mountain in it, which is us. We as the Ecclesia will take our rightful place and through governing with Jesus set Kingdom rule in order over nations. This is what Jesus said we would do in Matthew 28:19-20.

> Go therefore and make disciples of all the nations,
> baptizing them in the name of the Father and of the
> Son and of the Holy Spirit, teaching them to observe
> all things that I have commanded you; and lo, I am
> with you always, even to the end of the age." Amen
> (Matthew 28:19-20).

We are commissioned to disciple nations. We are not just to make disciples **in** nations, we are to disciple the nations themselves until they reflect a Kingdom culture. We are here to make nations look more like Heaven than like hell. We are here to turn nations from goat nations to sheep nations. (Matthew 25:31)

The way this is done is through the Church or house with a mountain in it operating with Jesus to judge nations. The word judge always speaks of judicial activity. Through judicial activity in the court of Heaven we set in place legal precedents that take away every right of demonic principalities to rule and influence nations. Once this is done we are then able to remove these powers and their influence over nations. These nations are freed to respond to the Gospel of the Kingdom and become expressions of His love, kindness and mercy. Justice will prevail and the people of these nations will be blessed because the cruelty of the devil and his forces is legally and then functionally removed.

This all happens from the Mountain named Zion. We have come to Mount Zion. In Mount Zion is the court/judicial system of Heaven. When you read Hebrews 12:22-24, everything mentioned is of legal nature.

> But you have come to Mount Zion and to the city of the living God, the Heavenly Jerusalem, to an innumerable company of angels, to the general assembly and church of the firstborn who are registered in Heaven, to God the Judge of all, to the spirits of just men made perfect, to Jesus the Mediator of the new covenant, and to the blood of sprinkling that speaks better things than that of Abel (Hebrews 12:22-24).

God is revealed as the Judge, Jesus is the Mediator, the blood is speaking and testifying because everything here is part of the court system of Heaven. When we come to Mount Zion, we come to the legal system of Heaven where nations are judged. In this place God is granted the legal right to fulfill His passion. We, the Ecclesia, are to be the house with the mountain in it. We are a part of this system and function.

Hebrews 12:22-24 lists the voices within the court system of Heaven. There are eight voices mentioned that we can encounter in the courts of Heaven and are to come into agreement with. There is one more voice in the courts mentioned elsewhere. There are a total of nine voices we are to learn to function within the court system. When we come into agreement with these voices, we become a part of granting God the legal right to fulfill His passion.

A dear apostolic friend said to me recently that God had spoken to him to agree with the intercession of Heaven. I believe that these voices represent the intercession of Heaven and it is with these, that we need to come into agreement. When we do, we grant God the evidence to render verdicts and judgments in agreement with His Kingdom will. We have been given a great privilege as His Ecclesia to function in the courts and win verdicts from Heaven that free nations to come under Kingdom domain.

We will study these voices in a reverse order from how they are spoken of in Scripture. The nine voices in the courts of Heaven include:

1. **The voice of the blood of Jesus.** The blood of Jesus releases testimony before the Throne of God that allows the Lord legal right to fulfill His passion.

2. **The Mediator of the new covenant.** Mediators are officers of a legal system sent to resolve conflict.

3. **The spirit of just men made perfect.** This speaks of those who are a part of the Church who have died and are in Heaven. They still have a viable and necessary function in the court system of Heaven.

4. **God, the Judge of all.** Isn't it interesting that God is revealed not as Father or Lord but as Judge in this Scripture. It is because the Holy Spirit desires us to recognize the legal position God holds as Judge of all.

5. **The Church of the firstborn registered in Heaven.** We as the Ecclesia have a tremendous place in the courts when we have been authorized and recognized.

6. **The general assembly.** The word in the Greek is universal companionship and it speaks of the multitudes worshipping the Lord about His throne. Their function of worship is essential to the operation of the courts.

7. **An innumerable company of angels.** There are varying ranks of angels that are a part of the court of Heaven's operations.

8. **The city of the living God, Heavenly Jerusalem.** This is actually the wife of the Lamb as is mentioned in the book of Revelation. The wife or Bride of the Lamb's voice has a tremendous impact in the courts of Heaven.

9. **The voice of finance.** Our giving of finances has great weight and authority when they come into agreement with Heaven's desire and intent.

We will look at each of these voices and their effect in the courts of Heaven in the next chapters. When we learn how to come into agreement with these voices, verdicts are rendered from the court so God's will is done in the Earth. There is nothing that cannot be accomplished when we get legal things in place. Once the legal issues are resolved and the devil's rights revoked, God is free to functionally take back the planet through His church. When we as the Church have come to Mount Zion and are ready to agree with the voices of Heaven, the result will be unprecedented breakthrough and victory.

6

The Testimony of the Blood

A lady told me a story of her daughter, living in another State, who was charged with attempted murder. It seemed that she and her husband had had a fight one evening. He left in one car while she jumped in the other family car and pursued him. She eventually rammed his car with her car. The police were called and because of the circumstances surrounding the incident, she was arrested and charged with attempted murder. As time progressed the husband and wife reconciled, but the District Attorney in the county where they lived, persisted in keeping the charges alive and pushing toward the court date. As the date loomed for the beginning of the trial, this mother approached me and asked if we could take this situation before the court of Heaven. I agreed and we set a date to meet and do this the day before the jury selection began.

As we began the process of coming before the court of Heaven, I led the lady in submitting herself to the Lord and His authority. We then brought her daughter and the entire situation before the court. I had a couple of seer prophets working with me to help discern what was going on in the courts of Heaven. As we began to pray I asked the lady to take her place as mother and intercessor and repent for her daughter. We began to sense very distinctly what the accuser was using against this young lady that was about to go on trial. The mom repented, with tears, as specifically as she could for her daughter's disobedience and rebellion. It wasn't very long before we felt the accusations had been dealt with before the court of Heaven. The accuser had been silenced and we were now free to ask the Lord for mercy. As we did this, the seers clearly heard and saw that the judge in the case would dismiss the case and it wouldn't even go to trial. We believed that the court of Heaven had made a ruling in favor of this lady's daughter.

The next afternoon I got a call from a very excited mom who reported that when the jury selection was about to begin, the judge in the case looked at the evidence and abruptly dismissed the case. The young woman was released from all charges and was free to resume her life after months of torment and uncertainty.

The court of Heaven had ruled and it was played out on Earth in a natural court. This all happened because of the testimony of the blood of Jesus on behalf of this lady's daughter. The blood had answered every accusation against this daughter and silenced the accuser that had demanded destruction. The accuser has no answer for the blood of Jesus. Therefore God the judge of all was granted the legal right to show mercy because of the blood.

A judge can only render verdicts on the basis of testimony given. Even though he may want to find in favor of another, he, from his position of justice, can only render verdicts based on what is testified. So it is in the courts of Heaven with God as the Supreme Judge of all. The judgments that come from the throne are always just and in agreement with the testimony presented in the courts. The nine voices that I have listed in the last chapter are voices that are testifying in the court of Heaven and are giving the Lord the legal right to fulfill His desire and passion. I believe that the blood of Jesus is the major voice in the court that testifies and has audience before God.

Revelation 12:10-11 tells us the accuser is overcome by the blood of Jesus.

> Then I heard a loud voice saying in heaven, "Now salvation, and strength, and the kingdom of our God, and the power of His Christ have come, for the accuser of our brethren, who accused them before our God day and night, has been cast down. And they overcame him by the blood of the Lamb and by the word of their testimony, and they did not love their lives to the death (Revelation 12:10-11).

When we learn how to come into agreement with the testimony of the blood of Jesus we find great power for redemption. The blood is not only testifying for our forgiveness and redemption but also for the redemption of the whole Earth. Nations will be redeemed because of the blood of Jesus. Agreement with the blood allows us to sense the passion that God has for nations. But it is the blood of Jesus that gets Kingdom verdicts from God's throne.

Blood has a Voice

All blood has a voice and speaks. We see this in the case of Cain killing Abel. In Genesis 4:8-12 we see Abel's blood getting a verdict from the Throne of God.

> Now Cain talked with Abel his brother; and it came to pass, when they were in the field, that Cain rose up against Abel his brother and killed him
> Then the Lord said to Cain, "Where is Abel your brother?"

He said, "I do not know. Am I my brother's keeper?"

And He said, "What have you done? The voice of your brother's blood cries out to Me from the ground. So now you are cursed from the earth, which has opened its mouth to receive your brother's blood from your hand. When you till the ground, it shall no longer yield its strength to you. A fugitive and a vagabond you shall be on the earth" (Genesis 4:8-12).

The Lord said that the blood of Abel was crying out to Him from the ground. Based on what Abel's blood was testifying, God renders judgment and a sentence against Cain. He was sentenced to be a vagabond and wanderer for the remainder of his days. The sentence was on the basis of the blood of Abel's testimony. The testimony of blood is very powerful before God's throne.

The High Priest would go behind the veil once a year on the Day of Atonement. He would sprinkle and pour out the blood of the Passover lamb. On the basis of the testimony of that blood, God would render a verdict that the sins of a nation were rolled back for one more year. The animal's blood could only release testimony that allowed God to be merciful for one year at a time. But when Jesus spilt His blood and poured and sprinkled it at the real altar in Heaven, the testimony of that blood allows God the legal right to forgive sins forever. Based on the testimony of Jesus' blood God now has legal right to be merciful and forgive sins and secure destinies forever.

To further help us understand the voice of blood, let me share a very personal story that happened when I was seeking to cleanse my bloodline. Everyone needs to have their bloodline cleansed. If the devil/accuser cannot find grounds to accuse us based on our behavior, he will search our bloodline to discover something to use against us in the heavenly court. This search is all the more diligent as we become an increasing threat to the powers of darkness. I have previously shared some of my experiences of how this affected my family and me personally. It is imperative to cleanse the bloodline so we can win victories in the court, but also not suffer a backlash from the devil and his forces.

We must realize that the cleansing of our bloodline should be done on a regular basis. If you were to look at your family tree you would discover that, as one person said to me, "It actually looks more like a jungle than a tree." Your history and ancestry have many branches and offshoots to it. Satan will search everything out to find any legal place to resist you in the courts of Heaven. Consistent cleansing of your bloodline keeps the devil from exploiting the sins of your forefathers against you and His Kingdom will.

As my bloodline was being cleansed another time, the seer prophets helping in this process saw that an ancestor of mine had been burned at the stake by Native American Indians. This ancestor cursed the Indians as he died. It was discerned by those who were seeing this, that the reason for this occurrence was my ancestor had stolen the Indian's land. As this was revealed I began to repent for what my forefathers had done. I repented for all the maliciousness and thievery against this Indian nation.

As I was doing this a prophet friend of mine was in the room. He was sitting next to me on the couch. I was aware that as I was walking through this scenario, he got up and moved away from me. As we concluded the session of repentance and the cleansing of my bloodline, I asked my prophet friend why he moved during the process. His response startled me. He said,

"I could feel the violence coming from your blood." My blood was speaking a violent thing as it was being cleansed. My literal blood in my veins had a voice of violence.

As this was said, I realized at least one of the reasons why I had struggled against anger in my life, especially in my earlier years. The anger that was in me had its roots in my blood that was defiled by the sins of my past generations. My blood had anger in it. Through the cleansing of my bloodline, not only was the legal right removed that the devil was using to resist me, but my blood was cleansed from the improper voice that it had.

The Cry of Jesus' Blood

All blood has a voice. Jesus' blood in the courts of Heaven has the greatest voice. His blood cries out for our forgiveness and redemption. We know this because as He was dying on the cross, He spoke forgiveness to all who would receive it. Luke 23:33-34 shows Jesus releasing forgiveness even as He is being crucified.

> And when they had come to the place called Calvary, there they crucified Him, and the criminals, one on the right hand and the other on the left. Then Jesus said, "Father, forgive them, for they do not know what they do" (Luke 23:33-34).

This is the cry of Jesus' blood. He is crying and testifying and granting the evidence of His blood before the courts of Heaven as the reason for our redemption. But Jesus blood also is testifying for more than just our salvation. The sacrifice of Jesus' blood also purchased all of creation back to God. Jesus blood is also crying out and granting God the legal right as Judge to secure all the Earth back under His Kingdom rule. We need to understand how large a sacrifice Jesus made on the cross and what it legally did. His sacrifice has legally secured nations back to the rule of God. Isaiah 49:6 says that the Father prophesied to Jesus that He would be salvation to the ends of the Earth.

> "Indeed He says,
> 'It is too small a thing that You should be My Servant
> To raise up the tribes of Jacob,
> And to restore the preserved ones of Israel;
> I will also give You as a light to the Gentiles,
> That You should be My salvation to the ends of the
> earth'" (Isaiah 49:6).

The Father said that Jesus' sacrifice was too great for just Israel's salvation. His sacrifice demanded that all the nations of the Earth would be redeemed. The blood of Jesus before the Throne of God is crying for nations to be redeemed. His blood is not just crying for the people in nations, but also the government of nations to function in a Kingdom culture.

Jesus' blood will not be silent until all that He bought at the cross is legally appropriated and set in place as a reality in the Earth. It is our job to agree with the testimony of the blood of Jesus until nations reflect His passion. His blood is legal testimony in the courts of Heaven for this.

The Church/Ecclesia must engage in and agree with the testimony of Jesus' blood. We are the stewards of His sacrifice in the Earth. We are to agree and add our testimony before the courts of Heaven for nations to be redeemed. Anything less than discipling nations, is an insult to the cross of Jesus. His blood is crying for this and we must set ourselves in agreement. The same passion that is carried in His blood must be in us.

The Moravians of centuries ago were a people sold out to the Lord. Many of them would sell themselves into slavery in foreign lands. Travelling as slaves, on slave ships, they headed to their new destination. They did this so that they could reach unevangelized people groups. They had a passion to reach the world with the gospel of Jesus Christ. What a commitment to the Lord and His Kingdom. As they were loading themselves on these ships they would sing a song. The words to this song are:

> I lay my life down
> I lay my self down
> I lay my crowns down at Your feet
>
> To win for the Lamb the rewards of His suffering
> To win for the Lamb the lost
> To win for the Lamb the rewards of His suffering
> And take up the cross

What a pure view of a people who had been possessed by the passion of the Lord. They had been overtaken by a passion and voice contained in the blood of Jesus. His blood is crying out for nations and all people groups to know Him in His power and glory.

The Blood of the Martyrs

There is one other aspect of the testimony of blood. As I have said, Jesus' blood is the predominant voice in the courts. But there is the voice of other people's blood that is also crying out and giving testimony in the courts of Heaven. Revelation 6:9-11 tells of the voice of the martyrs who gave their blood for a Kingdom cause while alive in the Earth.

> When He opened the fifth seal, I saw under the altar
> the souls of those who had been slain for the word
> of God and for the testimony which they held. And
> they cried with a loud voice, saying, "How long,
> O Lord, holy and true, until You judge and avenge
> our blood on those who dwell on the earth?" Then a
> white robe was given to each of them; and it was said
> to them that they should rest a little while longer,
> until both the number of their fellow servants and
> their brethren, who would be killed as they were,
> was completed (Revelation 6:9-11).

These martyrs are crying out for the 'avenging' of their
blood. We could look at this and think they are crying out for
someone to be punished for the spilling of their blood. Perhaps
this is so, but I believe that what they are really desiring and
communicating is their desire for what they spilt their blood for,
to matter. In other words if they laid down their lives before the
Lord so people and nations could be redeemed, their blood is
still crying in the courts of Heaven for this. Blood never stops
crying. Remember it has the power to get verdicts from the
throne of Heaven. This is shown in Revelation 12:11.

> And they overcame him by the blood of the Lamb
> and by the word of their testimony, and they did not
> love their lives to the death (Revelation 12:11).

When someone doesn't love their lives unto death, the accuser
has no power against them. The accusations of the accuser have
no power against this person and their testimony. They have

now won a great testimony before the courts of heaven. This is what Hebrews, chapter 11:1-2 declares.

> Now faith is the substance of things hoped for, the evidence of things not seen. For by it the elders obtained a good testimony (Hebrews 11:1-2).

Through living in faith and laying their lives down, the elders obtained a good testimony. This means they are still speaking before the courts of Heaven because they loved not their lives unto death, but laid them down for the sake of the Kingdom. When anyone does this, their blood has a voice in the courts of Heaven. It is crying out and testifying for what it was spilt for, to become a reality in the Earth. These under the Throne in Revelation 6 want what they gave their life for, to matter. Their blood is still speaking in the courts of Heaven to this end.

It is our job as individuals to come into agreement with the blood of Jesus in the courts. We must use the blood for our justification, we must agree with the blood for the nations it was given for and we must let the passion of the blood's voice impact and empower us. When we do, we become qualified to operate in the courts of Heaven and see verdicts rendered that grants God the legal right to fulfill His will.

The Lord is looking for the ones who will stand in their place and grant Him legal precedents to put in place the legalities of the cross. When this occurs, principalities are silenced and legal things come to order.

The reason nations are not being won to the Lord is because principalities and powers have a legal right through the sins of generations to hold them. They give witness in the courts of Heaven based on this legal right God, as Judge of all, cannot violate His own law and just take from these demonic powers their hold. The reason they have the domination must legally be removed. The legal removal of their rights is when our sins and the sins of the fathers are cleansed away by the blood of Jesus. When we repent of these sins and ask for the blood to cleanse, the legal right of principalities that are ruling nations is revoked from the courts of Heaven. Once their legal right is annulled, we can them rebuke them and they will flee. No amount of binding, loosing, rebuking or decreeing will work until the legal reason they are dominating is taken way. This is what the blood of Jesus does for us and the Kingdom purpose of God. Our requests, which up to now have been resisted, can then be granted and nations can come under Kingdom influence. The blood of Jesus is powerful. Let's use it and agree with it until Heaven invades Earth.

102

7

The Mediator's Testimony

I have a friend who found himself being <u>sued</u> for the fulfillment of a contract his company had signed. The company had agreed to pay this person a salary of $42,000. The problem was that the company that had been started, floundered and went out of business. This person, who was demanding payment, had been the person responsible for making the startup company a success. He obviously didn't do his job but was still demanding payment. As the day of the court date approached the judge in the matter ordered that both parties had to go before a 'mediator' to see if something could be worked out before they appeared in his courtroom. This was done and a solution was agreed upon by both parties. They then appeared before the judge for him simply to put his stamp on it and authorize it as legal.

The purpose of a mediator is to bring parties together into a place of agreement. Mediators and mediation is a legal function. The Bible says in Hebrews 12:24 that we have a mediator of the New Covenant.

> To Jesus the Mediator of the new covenant, and to the blood of sprinkling that speaks better things than that of Abel (Hebrews 12:24).

We have come to Jesus as the Mediator of the New Covenant. Jesus is the One who is standing in the courts of Heaven as the

Heavenly Mediator bringing God the Father and man together in agreement. The Scripture says the Man, Jesus, is the mediator. 1 Timothy 2:5 says that Jesus in His humanity and His Godhood stands as the mediator between God and us.

> For there is one God and one Mediator between God and men, the Man Christ Jesus (1 Timothy 2:5).

The thing that makes one a mediator is that he or she is 'fair' with both parties. A mediator has to be able to see where each party stands. As God, Jesus understands the demands of holiness, purity and righteousness. These standards cannot be compromised and are non-negotiable. God as God can never allow His righteousness to be compromised. The demand of God upon man is be holy as I am holy. 1 Peter 1:15-16 shows us this demand.

> But as He who called you is holy, you also be holy in all your conduct, because it is written, "Be holy, for I am holy" (1 Peter 1:15-16).

God has never lessened His demands on Man. He just answered them in and through Jesus Christ. In addition, He grants us the grace that empowers us to live holy lives as He is holy. If and when we fail, there is forgiveness for us through Jesus Christ. I John 2:1 tells us that we are to strive not to sin, but should we sin, what Jesus accomplished on the cross grants God the legal right to forgive us.

> My little children, these things I write to you, so that you may not sin. And if anyone sins, we have an

Advocate with the Father, Jesus Christ the righteous
(1 John 2:1).

Jesus is in the courts of Heaven as our Mediator bringing God
and us together so what legally needs to happen can. Not only
does Jesus as Mediator stand for the demands of God in holiness,
but He also stands as Man understanding our frailty. He lived
as a man and understands the pressures and temptations of our
humanity. Scripture says, Jesus was tempted and yet did not
sin. Hebrews 4:15-16 encourages us with the fact that Jesus
understands where we live and what we war against.

> For we do not have a High Priest who cannot
> sympathize with our weaknesses, but was in all
> points tempted as we are, yet without sin. Let us
> therefore come boldly to the throne of grace, that
> we may obtain mercy and find grace to help in time
> of need (Hebrews 4:15-16).

When the Bible says Jesus was tempted this means He felt the
pull and enticement of sin. It was real. Yet from the power of
the Holy Spirit and the grace He supplied, Jesus said "No"
to sin every time. Because of this He has won a place in the
courts of Heaven greater than any other place. It also means
He understands the limits on our humanity. Because of this He
is qualified to stand as our Mediator with God and as God's
Mediator with us.

Notice the reason for Jesus' mediation is concerning the
New Covenant. He is the mediator of the New Covenant. The
term 'covenant' is a legal term as well. Anytime God made
covenant with man, he came into a legal agreement. He was

promising on the basis of covenant that He would fulfill His Word and promises connected to that covenant. Jesus as our Mediator and God's Mediator is working to remove every hindrance from our getting the promises of the New Covenant. There are many promises connected to the New Covenant. This covenant is based on better promises and a better sacrifice. Hebrews 8:6 says that the covenant Jesus is mediating is based on better promises.

> But now He has obtained a more excellent ministry, inasmuch as He is also Mediator of a better covenant, which was established on better promises (Hebrews 8:6).

Jesus is here to mediate into place everything that is legally ours by virtue of His cross and sacrifice. God made promises based on Jesus' blood and sacrifice. These promises are ours in Jesus. They belong to us. But our own weakness and humanity work against us from getting these promises.

The accuser will resist us from getting the promises contained in the New Covenant. Jesus by His blood and sacrifice as our Mediator is working to answer every accusation so we can legally have what was legally bought and paid for at the cross. Anything that we have yet to get from the sacrifice of the cross is because something legal is being used by the devil to resist it. Jesus, as Mediator, is working to remove this so we can have all that Jesus paid for us to have. If we have prayed and have yet to get what is legally ours from the cross, we must operate in discernment before the courts of Heaven to remove what hinders us. Our Mediator is operating on our behalf as well.

Our Mediator, Jesus, is presenting before the courts of

Heaven our legal claims based on what He accomplished on the cross. The accuser of the brethren is pointing out in the courts why God cannot legally grant what Jesus bought and paid for. The accuser bases his accusation out of the holiness of the Lord. Before God can legally grant what Jesus purchased for us and is ours by covenant, the Mediator must answer these accusations in the courts. This usually requires our repentance and a putting into place of the blood of Jesus for our sins. Remember the devil has no answer for the blood. When we truly repent of our sins the blood cleanses them away and also takes away the right of the devil to resist us. We are now free to receive of the promises of the New Covenant.

One of the ways the mediator operates in the courts of Heaven in our behalf is through His testimony. Revelation 19:10 gives us a very interesting insight into Jesus releasing testimony as our Mediator.

> And I fell at his feet to worship him. But he said to me, "See that you do not do that! I am your fellow servant, and of your brethren who have the testimony of Jesus. Worship God! For the testimony of Jesus is the spirit of prophecy" (Revelation 19:10).

John the Apostle makes a mistake in worshipping someone sent with a message. This was not an angel because he says he is his fellow servant and of his brothers. This one was of the Great Cloud of witnesses I assume. We will touch this later. This man then grants John revelation. He says the testimony of Jesus is the spirit of prophecy. When Jesus as Mediator is testifying in the courts of Heaven, it can become prophecy in the mouth of us here on Earth. As we prophesy, we are agreeing and releasing the same testimony that Jesus is releasing in the courts of Heaven.

Prophecy isn't just information in the Earth realm. Prophecy is agreeing with the testimony of Jesus in the courts of Heaven. This is why every word will be established in the mouth of two or three witnesses. 2 Corinthians 13:1 says that things are established and considered to be true where more than one witness has said the same thing.

> This will be the third time I am coming to you. "By the mouth of two or three witnesses every word shall be established" (2 Corinthians 13:1).

This Scripture refers to court proceedings. When we prophesy we should be speaking what Jesus is testifying. Our voice in the courts agreeing with the voice of the Mediator grants God evidence to release verdicts in our behalf. The promises of the New Covenant are then free to come into the Earth realm.

To understand Jesus as the Mediator we need to know that *mediator* is an all-inclusive term of Jesus' function in the courts of Heaven. I have briefly explained what a mediator is. There are others terms associated with this term of mediator. Jesus is called High Priest, Intercessor and Advocate as our Mediator.

Jesus the High Priest

As High Priest, it is Jesus' responsibility to present an offering that grants God the legal right to show mercy and not judgment. This is the basic function of the High Priest. This is what Aaron did as High Priest. Through the offerings he presented, God was then free to be merciful to a people He would otherwise have had to judge. The good news is that not only is Jesus the High Priest, he is also the offering that He as High Priest offers. His sacrifice and offering is sufficient for God legally to forgive, save and redeem us into our destinies. Hebrews 9:11-12 show us that Jesus' sacrifice gave Him something as High Priest to offer.

> But Christ came as High Priest of the good things to come, with the greater and more perfect tabernacle not made with hands, that is, not of this creation. Not with the blood of goats and calves, but with His own blood He entered the Most Holy Place once for all, having obtained eternal redemption (Hebrews 9:11-12).

Jesus as High Priest offered His own blood in the Most Holy Place to grant God the legal right to bless us, save us and redeem us into our destinies. This is the function of the High Priest. Even though Jesus as High Priest operates here, we have to appropriate this activity as believers. This requires faith and repentance in what Jesus has, and is, doing. We must understand that Jesus has finished the work of redemption but is still active in the courts of Heaven until all He has done becomes reality in our lives. Jesus, from a place of rest, is now waiting until we, the Ecclesia, embrace and activate all He has done. Hebrews 10:12-13 show us that Jesus' present activity is from a place of rest.

> But this Man, after He had offered one sacrifice for sins forever, sat down at the right hand of God, from that time waiting till His enemies are made His footstool (Hebrews 10:12-13).

When Scripture says that Jesus has sat down, it doesn't imply inactivity. Sitting down speaks of a place of absolute dominion and rulership. From this place He is waiting for His people, the Ecclesia to work with Him to put into place all that He legally purchased and paid for. He is still active from this place of dominion. When the Bible speaks of 'rest' it is not speaking just of peace. It is speaking of a position of dominion and rulership. This is what Hebrews 4:9 says, *"There remains therefore a rest for the people of God"*, even though it has been spoken of since creation. God is not waiting on a people just to have peace. He is waiting on a people to enter His position of dominion and rule from that place. He is waiting on us to discover and find the place of rulership with Him that He always desired.

When God made Adam on the sixth day, Adam arose on the seventh day and said to God, "What are we going to do today?" God responded, "Nothing. I want you to learn immediately that everything we are going to do, we are going to do from rest."

We do not accomplish the will of God from striving. We accomplish the will of God through resting in Him. Remember 'rest' is not inactivity. Rest is working from a position of dominion and absolute authority. This is what Jesus is doing. He is still operating as Mediator, High Priest, Intercessor and Advocate. All of these things He is doing are from a position of rest and rulership.

Jesus - The Intercessor

As our High Priest, Jesus is functioning in the courts of Heaven as our Intercessor. Hebrews 7:25 shows that Jesus is interceding for us.

> Therefore He is also able to save to the uttermost those who come to God through Him, since He always lives to make intercession for them (Hebrews 7:25).

Jesus ever lives to make intercession for us. Intercession is a legal activity. When we intercede, we are granting God the legal right to intervene in a situation. Through our intercession we are putting things legally into place for God to win. If God loses, it is because something legal has not been dealt with by us. Intercession is always made on the basis of an offering. If there is no offering then there is no basis for intercession. But where there is an offering, God remembers us. Psalm 20:1-4 shows us that God blessed and remembered them on the basis of their offerings.

> May the Lord answer you in the day of trouble;
> May the name of the God of Jacob defend you;
> May He send you help from the sanctuary,
> And strengthen you out of Zion;
> May He remember all your offerings,
> And accept your burnt sacrifice.
>   Selah
> May He grant you according to your heart's desire,
> And fulfill all your purpose (Psalm 20:1-4).

The Psalmist is speaking of how God will defend, help and strengthen us. Then he says, *"May He remember all your offerings and burnt sacrifices."* It is offerings that create the basis by which we are heard.

Jesus as our Intercessor also needs an offering to form the basis on which His prayer is heard. His body and His blood, which He offered on the Cross are His offering. If Jesus didn't give His body and blood as an offering, He could not be our Intercessor. Hebrews 7:25-27 shows us that Jesus' function as Intercessor is connected to the offering of Himself that He made. Because of this sacrifice that is on the altar, His intercession has power and is legally accepted.

> Therefore He is also able to save to the uttermost
> those who come to God through Him, since He
> always lives to make intercession for them. For
> such a High Priest was fitting for us, who is holy,
> harmless, undefiled, separate from sinners, and has
> become higher than the Heavens; who does not need
> daily, as those high priests, to offer up sacrifices,
> first for His own sins and then for the people's, for
> this He did once for all when He offered up Himself
> (Hebrews 7:25-27).

This is good news for us. We should also have gifts on the altar.
Our financial giving, sacrifices and offerings of ourselves create
a basis for us to pray and intercede. Even if all that we have is the
offering of Jesus' blood and body, we have a legal right to stand
in the courts of the Lord. The truth is that Jesus as Intercessor
has a right to be heard in Heaven because of His offering. This
is true for us as well. Abel was heard and accepted because
of his offering. Hebrews 11:4 says that God testified of Abel's
offering.

> By faith Abel offered to God a more excellent
> sacrifice than Cain, through which he obtained
> witness that he was righteous, God testifying of
> his gifts; and through it he being dead still speaks
> (Hebrews 11:4).

God gave witness that Abel was righteous because He testified
of his gifts. In other words, the Lord from His throne, deemed
Abel righteous based on the faith gifts he brought to the Lord.

The Scripture goes on to say that he is still speaking today. I personally believe that his extravagant giving and offerings granted him a place of intercession still being heard today.

Jesus as our Intercessor is interceding on the basis of His sacrifice for us. His intercession is in agreement with what His blood is speaking. It has great power in the courts of Heaven as we agree.

Jesus - Our Advocate

The last thing that Jesus being our Mediator means is He is our Advocate. 1 John 2:1-2 shows us that we have an advocate with the Father, Jesus Christ the Righteous.

> My little children, these things I write to you, so that you may not sin. And if anyone sins, we have an Advocate with the Father, Jesus Christ the righteous. And He Himself is the propitiation for our sins, and not for ours only but also for the whole world (1 John 2:1-2).

As our Advocate, Jesus is our intercessor, comforter and consoler. From His righteous position in the courts of Heaven, we have imputed righteousness. When we fail or sin, God will forgive us for Jesus' sake and impute His righteousness to us so we can stand legally in the courts of Heaven. This only occurs if we repent. We must really repent and turn away from sin. Once this is done, we are positioned in the courts of Heaven to be a part of the process. This is what 2 Corinthians 5:21 says,

> For He made Him who knew no sin to be sin for us, that we might become the righteousness of God in

Him (2 Corinthians 5:21).

We are the righteousness of God in Christ Jesus. We, by faith, repent and receive the imputed righteousness that comes from the Lord Jesus Christ and His sacrifice. This is what allows us to stand in the courts of the Lord. Again, the accuser has no answer for the blood.

Jesus is our Advocate and will comfort and console us when we fail. He will also chasten us and press us to greater holiness. His grace doesn't just forgive us; His grace empowers us to overcome sin.

To illustrate this, let me share an event from my own personal life. Several years ago Mary and I took our 6 children on a vacation to a resort in Mexico. It was one of the resorts where you paid a price and then all the food, lodging and some activities were then available to you. This was a big thing for our family of 8. We did not have a lot of money and felt privileged to be able to do this as a family. I think it was the second night that I had a dream. In my dream Jesus came to me. He didn't look like Jesus. In fact He looked like a well-known actor, yet I knew it was Jesus without question. Jesus said to me, "You have grieved the Father". The moment He said this I knew exactly what I had been doing that had grieved the Lord. I began to weep in the dream. Jesus turned to go back to the Father and I reached out to touch Him as He was leaving. He stopped and turned back to me. I then said to Him, "Is this going to cause me to lose my destiny". I was very broken over what I had been told. Jesus then looked at me and said, "I did not come to tell you this so you would be overcome, I came to tell you this so you would overcome". I then awoke.

When I woke up everything in me wanted to discard this dream as not being the Lord because of who Jesus looked like.

I didn't want to hear the message Jesus had brought me. But I knew it was the Lord. I believe the reason Jesus chose to look like someone that I didn't think He would look like, was to see if I would hear truth from Him in whatever form He brought it. Mark 16:12 says Jesus appeared to them in another form. They wouldn't recognize Him except by the Spirit. We have to be able to hear Him and receive from Him even when we would like to disregard the message. I did however embrace the message He brought. I knew this was in agreement with the Word of God. Jesus was acting as my Advocate with the Father. He came to tell me what the Father's posture was toward me at that present moment, but also how to correct it. I did get past the pain of the chastisement and overcome what could have destroyed my future and destiny. It was because of Jesus' operation and function as my Advocate that empowered me to do this. As Advocate, He not only brought comfort, but also pressed me to overcome and go to new realms of holiness.

The longer we walk with Jesus, the more we learn to say no to sin. Even on our best days of walking before Him and with Him, I still need His righteousness imputed to me. This is what grants me authority and place in the courts of Heaven. I do not come on my own merit, but on the merit of who He is and what He has done for me. The Father will receive us for Jesus sake, if we repent and grab hold of His provisions for forgiveness and His power to walk in holiness. We cannot excuse our sin. Everything that is necessary for us to overcome has been provided. May we not grieve the Father, but please Him and His heart. Our Advocate waits to help us into this life of empowerment and overcoming.

Jesus' voice as Mediator is speaking in the courts of Heaven. From this voice and agreement with this voice there is testimony released that grants God the legal right to fulfill

His passion. When we understand this, we do not have to pull back in shame. We walk forward in true repentance receiving the forgiveness of the Lord, taking our place before His throne of grace. When we do, judicial activity comes from the court that grants God the legal right to invade the planet. May we be a part of this process.

8

The Testimony of Just Men Made Perfect

A young man who is a close friend of our family found himself in legal trouble. He became involved in a fight (started by the other person) and during the fight, he broke the man's jaw. The long and short of it was that this young man was found guilty of a misdemeanor assault charge and placed on probation. Instead of being diligent to take care of the things required concerning his probation, he left the State.

About two years later, his wife took a teaching job that required them to live in this State again. The problem was that he had violated the terms of his parole in this State and there was now a warrant out for his arrest. The young man wanted to set things in order. He did not want this hanging over his head as he knew it would be only a matter of time until he was stopped for a traffic violation or some other incident and he would be off to jail.

His lawyer therefore arranged a meeting with the District Attorney and they agreed to recommend to the judge that this young man should pay all the fines and penalties and spend 10 days in county jail. The judge could accept the recommendation or he could disregard it and set his own penalty.

On hearing of his situation, I began to tell him about the court of Heaven. I explained that he could appeal to the Lord who sits on the throne of grace to find mercy in his time of need. We had a 'court session' on behalf of his situation. I remember leading this young man through the process of answering accusations in the court of Heaven that were standing against him. The Spirit of the Lord came upon that time of prayer and the young man began to weep in repentance at the choices he had made and even the violence and anger that had been a part of his life. I sensed very clearly that a verdict came from the court that justified this young man and forgiveness and redemption flowed out of the courts of Heaven.

On the day of the actual court proceedings, the young man and his lawyer stood before a judge who had a reputation for being business-like and not given to extending mercy. As the lawyer presented the facts before the judge and the judge read the DA's recommendation, his countenance changed. The judge said that this seemed like a 'slap on the wrist' for two years of parole violation. It wasn't looking good for the young man.

The judge could sentence him to two years of jail time if he chose. Then suddenly with no input from anyone in the court, the judge looked at the young man and said, "Here's what I am going to do. I am going to suspend ALL jail time. I am going to let you continue your education. I am going to re-institute your driver's license, (it had been suspended) and I am going to allow you another chance to get this behind you." The judge granted more than was requested!

The court of Heaven had answered the plea of the young man and the verdict of Heaven manifested in a natural court. This happened because we went into the court of Heaven, silenced the accusations of the devil and received a sentence of mercy from God. If we can learn to function in the courts of Heaven and stop yelling at the devil, we will see life altered on the planet.

Thrones and the Court System

There is a very real court system in Heaven. Every time we read about the Throne of God in Heaven, we must understand that it is not simply referring to a place of worship, but also to the Judge's seat in the court system. The Throne of God is where the courts of Heaven operate. There is no clearer place we see this than in Daniel 7:9-10.

> I watched till thrones were put in place,
> And the Ancient of Days was seated;
> His garment was white as snow,
> And the hair of His head was like pure wool.
> His throne was a fiery flame,
> Its wheels a burning fire;
> A fiery stream issued
> And came forth from before Him.
> A thousand thousands ministered to Him;
> Ten thousand times ten thousand stood before Him.
> The court was seated,
> And the books were opened (Daniel 7:9-10).

What a powerful description of the throne of God. Notice that the throne of God is central to the court of Heaven and it is surrounded by many other thrones. The book of Revelation tells us that, apart from God's throne, there are at least 24 other thrones that also form part of the court system.

> Around the throne were twenty-four thrones, and on
> the thrones I saw twenty-four elders sitting, clothed
> in white robes; and they had crowns of gold on their
> heads (Revelation 4:4).

We see here that those who occupy these thrones have a crown on their heads and play a part in the court system of Heaven. They are humans that have overcome and won the right to take these thrones. We know this because of the crowns that they wear.

Crowns are for humans who have faithfully served the Lord and gained a place of authority in the Lord. This includes not only those who are presently in Heaven, but also those of us who are still alive in the Earth. You can be alive on Earth and still be a part of the court system of Heaven. In fact if we do not take our place in the courts of Heaven, God's plans for the planet cannot come to fruition. I often say that, in the natural, my feet may be on the floor, but in the spirit, I am standing in the courts of the Lord playing a vital purpose to His Kingdom cause.

2 Timothy 4:8 says that the Apostle Paul would wear a crown as well as others who loved the coming and appearing of the Lord.

> Finally, there is laid up for me the crown of righteousness, which the Lord, the righteous Judge, will give to me on that Day, and not to me only, but also to all who have loved His appearing (2 Timothy 4:8).

James 1:12 promises that a crown of life will be given to those who endure temptation and love the Lord.

> Blessed is the man who endures temptation; for when he has been approved, he will receive the crown of life which the Lord has promised to those who love Him (James 1:12).

My point is that those who overcome in this life win for themselves crowns and places in the court system of Heaven. Even Jesus won His place as High Priest and His other functions in the courts by virtue of His obedience to the Father.

I think it is clear that 12 of the 24 who are the elders that are wearing crowns in the courts of Heaven and occupying thrones are the original apostles. Jesus spoke to them in Luke 22:28-30.

> "But you are those who have continued with Me in My trials. And I bestow upon you a kingdom, just as My Father bestowed one upon Me, that you may eat and drink at My table in My kingdom, and sit on thrones judging the twelve tribes of Israel" (Luke 22:28-30).

Jesus promised these apostles that they would sit on twelve thrones judging the twelve tribes of Israel. Remember that judging is a judicial act. Notice also that these positions that Jesus refers to, are given as a result of their faithfulness to continue with Him in His tribulation. Again, positions within the courts are won not given.

The other 12 thrones that are mentioned in Revelation are probably occupied by representatives of the twelve tribes of Israel. This would be consistent with the order and language of Scripture. These 24 elders that occupy 24 thrones make up some of the thrones that are a part of the courts of Heaven.

The Great Cloud of Witnesses

I know that many people believe that Heaven is a place where we go to sit on clouds and play golden harps all day. This is absolutely untrue! Revelation 6:9-11 gives us a picture of some of the activity going on in Heaven.

> When He opened the fifth seal, I saw under the altar
> the souls of those who had been slain for the word
> of God and for the testimony which they held. And
> they cried with a loud voice, saying, "How long,
> O Lord, holy and true, until You judge and avenge
> our blood on those who dwell on the earth?" Then a
> white robe was given to each of them; and it was said
> to them that they should rest a little while longer,
> until both the number of their fellow servants and
> their brethren, who would be killed as they were,
> was completed (Revelation 6:9-11).

These martyrs (people who laid down their lives for the sake of
the Gospel) are still praying and interceding. They are crying
out for justice concerning their own blood that was spilled.
They are requesting that the reason for their sacrifice would
become a reality. There are many in the Heavenly realm who
are still crying and praying for what they spilt their blood for,
to be realized on the Earth. They are a part of the great cloud of
witnesses. Hebrews 11:39-40 and Hebrews 12:1-2 speak of this
great cloud of witnesses.

> And all these, having obtained a good testimony
> through faith, did not receive the promise, God having
> provided something better for us, that they should not
> be made perfect apart from us. Therefore we also, since
> we are surrounded by so great a cloud of witnesses, let
> us lay aside every weight, and the sin which so easily
> ensnares us, and let us run with endurance the race that
> is set before us (Hebrews 12:1-2).

This great cloud of witnesses has a role in the courts of Heaven. The word witness in Hebrews 12:1 speaks of those who give judicial testimony. The cloud of witnesses has a voice in the courts of the Lord concerning the Kingdom purposes for which they laid down their lives. Notice that they have a right to speak in the courts because they have won for themselves a good testimony, which is about judicial approval.

We need to understand that the saints of old are still invested in the causes for which they gave their lives. They are not just cheering us on from some celestial grand stand. They are actually in the courts releasing their voice and testimony on behalf of those of us who must now complete the work for which they gave their lives.

This is what the term spirits of just men made perfect refers to in Hebrews 12:23.

> To the general assembly and church of the firstborn who are registered in Heaven, to God the Judge of all, to the spirits of just men made perfect (Hebrews 12:23).

These saints of old still have a voice and are releasing testimony in the courts of Heaven. They have won a place in the courts because of their obedience to the Lord while on Earth.

The Church in Heaven and on Earth

As we function in the courts from the earthly realm, we are to come into agreement with the intercession of these witnesses. Our agreement with them produces the legal right for Heaven to fulfill the reason for which they laid down their lives. Whatever the reason was—spheres of society being won to the

Lord, geographical locations brought under Kingdom domain or nations discipled into a Kingdom culture—there must be legal precedents in place before it can be fulfilled. This will only happen when the Church that is on Earth and the Church that is in Heaven come into agreement for His Kingdom will to be done. Ephesians 3:14-15 shows us that there is one church, whether we are in Earth or already in Heaven.

> For this reason I bow my knees to the Father of our
> Lord Jesus Christ, from whom the whole family in
> Heaven and Earth is named (Ephesians 3:14-15).

Whether we are in Heaven or on Earth, we are one church. Together we are striving for one purpose and that is, to see Heaven invade the Earth and God's ultimate Kingdom agenda manifest. This church (in Heaven and Earth) must take its place in the court system of Heaven.

As I was about to teach on the great cloud of witnesses and their function in the courts of the Lord, my wife, Mary, had a dream. I had not told her what I was about to teach. I was actually afraid that she wouldn't be able to embrace it and, quite honestly, I was a little unsure of what I was about to share. When she had this dream with no knowledge of what I was about to teach, it got my attention.

In the dream my natural father (who had passed away 16 years before) came to her and communicated that he had not cared for the funeral service that we had held for him. He told Mary, in the dream, that he wanted another service. He explained that since he had been in Heaven, he had heard an African children's choir singing "O Happy Day". He now wanted another funeral service in which an African children's choir would sing "O

Happy Day". In the dream, plans were being made to 'redo' his funeral service to honor him appropriately.

When she told me this dream, I knew it was the Lord confirming to me what I was about to teach. I taught the lesson on the great cloud of witnesses. I told those who were present that the cloud of witnesses that were functioning in the courts of the Lord were to be honored for the sacrifice they had made for the Kingdom of God. I knew this was what was being communicated through Mary's dream about my Dad.

As the service ended, I played a clip of an African children's choir singing "O Happy Day." I did this in honor of my Dad and his life. Without his influence I would not be in the ministry today. I was honoring the legacy of my natural father and his place in the great cloud of witnesses. As we did this, a tremendous presence of the Lord filled the room and I knew it was the Lord bearing witness to the understanding that had been brought.

They Cannot Be Made Perfect Without Us

The great cloud of witnesses stand before the Throne of Heaven testifying and witnessing concerning God's Kingdom purposes still to be accomplished. The Bible clearly says that they, without us, cannot be made perfect. Hebrews 11:39-40 tells us that their ultimate passion cannot be fulfilled without us finishing and joining with their sacrifice to see God's agenda done.

> And all these, having obtained a good testimony through faith, did not receive the promise, God having provided something better for us, that they

should not be made perfect apart from us (Hebrews 11:39-40).

The great cloud of witnesses, obtained a good testimony and the right to speak in the courts of Heaven. Through their testimony, judgments can now be released from the throne that are instrumental in establishing God's will on Earth. The cloud of witnesses laid down their lives to see the Kingdom come on Earth and they remain invested in this mission until it becomes a reality. They, without us, cannot be made perfect.

Several years ago I had a dream that I was sitting at breakfast with Smith Wigglesworth, the great apostle of faith who had a tremendous healing ministry. I remember in the dream thinking that this man is dead, but yet here I am speaking with him as if he were alive. The thought I had was that I wanted him to pray for me before the 'meeting' was over. The dream ended before this could happen.

For years this dream intrigued me. What was the significance, if any, of me speaking with Smith Wigglesworth? A man who had already died and gone to Heaven? I now believe that Smith Wigglesworth is part of the great cloud of witnesses. My 'meeting' with him concerned something he carried in his ministry that I was to carry in mine. Could it be that he was actually interceding for me to come into the anointing that he carried for healing? Could it be that he was petitioning the courts of Heaven for a verdict that would allow me to walk in the same authority that he walked in as 'the apostle of faith'?

Many years later when I was in a meeting where seer prophets were present who saw into Heaven and the court system, one of them began to declare that Smith Wigglesworth was present and wanted to give me his anointing. I was flabbergasted! First, the dream and now a prophetic word. However, I am very careful with this kind of thing. I know that it is really easy to wander off into realms of delusion and even witchcraft. Yet I didn't want to miss anything that the Lord had for me.

The seer prophet, who is very humble, wanted to take her scarf that she had around her neck and place it as a mantle on my neck to symbolize the anointing of Smith Wigglesworth coming upon me. I submitted to this and to my amazement when the scarf was place around my neck an intense heat and fire went into my neck and down my back. I definitely received something from the Lord and have begun to walk in it. The cloud of witnesses is committed to helping us fulfill our assignments in our generations because without us, they will not be made perfect.

Here is a final story to illustrate the operation of the great cloud of witnesses in the courts of Heaven. A young man was terribly injured in a car accident. The doctors said that he should have died. Instead he was in a coma for an extended period of time. When he came out of this coma he told a very intriguing story. While in the coma, he found himself in the courtroom of Heaven. The issue being debated in the courts of Heaven was whether this young man should come on to Heaven or stay on Earth and fulfill what was written in the books of Heaven about him. He said there were several people that were giving their opinions and testimonies in the matter.

Suddenly a man walked into the courtroom. He had a long white beard, was very humble and began to testify as to why this young man should be allowed to stay on Earth and fulfill his destiny. On the basis of this man's testimony the court rendered a verdict that allowed the young man to live and finish his course. Now, remember, the young man in his comatose state is witnessing this whole process.

As the man with the long white beard turned to leave, the

young man called to him, "Sir, Sir, please stop, Sir." The man stopped and looked at this young man whose destiny on Earth had just been secured. As the man stopped, the young man said, "Sir, what is your name." The man responded, "My name is Noah." Wow! Some would have a real problem with this for various reasons. It does however align with the fact that there are spirits of just men made perfect that function in the courts of Heaven.

Even the Lord Himself spoke of Noah as one of three that were extreme intercessors that had won a place in the courts of Heaven. Ezekiel 14:14 lists Noah, Daniel and Job as ones that hold great authority as intercessors.

> Even if these three men, Noah, Daniel, and Job, were in it, they would deliver only themselves by their righteousness," says the Lord GOD (Ezekiel 14:14).

When God spoke these words, all of them were already dead and in Heaven, yet God refers to them as still functioning in intercession. Do they still hold place of function in the courts of Heaven as a part of the just men made perfect? I believe so. They are still a part of the activities of the court to help grant God the legal right to fulfill His Father's passion.

There is a very real cloud of witnesses in Heaven. They are a part of the court system of Heaven. They have a strategic function as witnesses in this judicial process. They cannot be made perfect without us. May we learn to flow in agreement with them for God's purposes to manifest on Earth.

9

The Voice of the Judge

The O. J. Simpson trial was hailed as The Trial of the Century. He was charged with the murder of his ex-wife, Nicole Simpson, and Ron Goldman. The outcome of the trial was that O. J. was found innocent of the crime and set free. This was a surprising verdict that is debated to this day. What I remember most clearly was the drama that surrounded the trial as evidence was presented by both prosecution and defense attorneys.

The Judge in that case was Lance Ito. Many have criticized his overseeing of the trial. They complain that he allowed into evidence things that should never have been allowed and that he was swayed by the publicity generated by this high profile trial. Regardless of all this, the fact remains that during the trial, Judge Ito had the final word.

The same is true in the courts of Heaven. The Judge who sits on the throne of the courts of Heaven has the final say. In the courts of Heaven there can be a multitude of witnesses, evidence being presented and cases being petitioned, but only the Judge of

Righteousness determines the verdict. His verdicts are always just and true. We see this in 1 Kings 22:19-23 when Micaiah begins to reveal what he saw in the courts of Heaven concerning Ahab and his destruction.

Then Micaiah said, "Therefore hear the word of the

> Lord: I saw the Lord sitting on His throne, and all the host of Heaven standing by, on His right hand and on His left. And the Lord said, 'Who will persuade Ahab to go up, that he may fall at Ramoth Gilead?' So one spoke in this manner, and another spoke in that manner. Then a spirit came forward and stood before the Lord, and said, 'I will persuade him.' The Lord said to him, 'In what way?' So he said, 'I will go out and be a lying spirit in the mouth of all his prophets.' And the Lord said, 'You shall persuade him, and also prevail. Go out and do so.' Therefore look! The Lord has put a lying spirit in the mouth of all these prophets of yours, and the Lord has declared disaster against you" (1 Kings 22:19-23).

As the Lord was hearing from the host of Heaven around the throne, there was a debate on how they could make Ahab fall. Ahab had led Israel into wickedness and the Lord was ready to judge him. The Scripture says that one said they could do it this way and another could do it that way. Then a spirit came forward during the proceedings and declared that he would go and be a lying spirit in the mouth of Ahab's prophets. The Lord on the throne passed a sentence. He said, "Go and prevail."

What an awesome glimpse into the court system of Heaven. In this Scripture, there are many voices in the court giving ideas and testimonies concerning what should be done. But when the Lord was ready to make the decision and pass judgment, it was The Lord who sits on the Throne as Judge Who rendered it. The Lord is the Righteous Judge Who does all things well.

Father and Judge

It is quite interesting in Hebrews 12:23 that the Lord is revealed as "The Judge of All."

> To the general assembly and church of the firstborn who are registered in Heaven, to God the Judge of all, to the spirits of just men made perfect (Hebrews 12:23).

He is not revealed as our Father, our Savior or our King. He is revealed as the Judge. The reason for this is that these Scriptures are revealing the court system of Heaven and He as Judge has the final word and place. He is in fact all the things previously mentioned and much more, but He is the Judge of All because He renders verdicts, judgments and sentences that bring order and justice.

I want to make a statement here that is at the core of this book. It is our job as individuals and the Ecclesia to grant God, as the Judge of all, the legal right to fulfill His fatherly passion. We should remember that God is a Father. In his heart, he carries dreams, desires and longings for His family, just as earthly fathers do. He longs to see these desires of His heart towards His family come to pass. God is also the Judge of all who must render legal judgments in righteousness and holiness. As we have discovered, there can be legal issues that hinder His fatherly desires being fulfilled. God will never compromise Himself as Judge in order to fulfill His fatherly desires. To do so would make Him less than God. Therefore, it is our job as His people, His Ecclesia, to put in place the legal precedents needed for God to legally fulfill His desires as a Father.

Removing the Legal Right of the Enemy

One of the best ways for me to explain this is through a personal experience. There was a lady very close to our family that was diagnosed with breast cancer. When this lady was 13 years old, her own mother had been diagnosed with breast cancer and she died at just 43 years of age. The disease had spread in her body just as it was now spreading in her daughter's body. This friend of ours was 43 when she was diagnosed and also had a 13 year old daughter. The parallels were astounding. I knew we were dealing with a generational, family curse.

When she was on her death-bed, her husband called me and asked if I would pray for her. I went to her home where there were already other people gathered at her bedside praying for her. I placed my hand on her head and as I began to pray I felt the Father's passion to heal this woman. It was unmistakable. I had felt this many times before in many situations and knew it well. I prayed the best prayer I knew how to pray. I prayed with the unction and power of the Spirit of the Lord. It wasn't a natural prayer, it was a supernatural one. Yet, twelve hours later, she died. She died at age 43, leaving behind a 13-year-old daughter – exactly as her mother had done! What a tragedy. It was only much later that I was able to explain why this had happened. At the time of my prayer, I did not know that this lady and her husband had connived to steal resources that belonged to someone else. This activity of dishonor and thievery had opened the door for the family curse to come upon her life.

Proverbs 26:2 says that a curse has to have a **cause** to alight.

Like a flitting sparrow, like a flying swallow, So a curse without cause shall not alight (Proverbs 26:2).

Curses are pictured as sparrows and swallows flying around and looking for a place to land. They cannot land unless a legal right allows them to land. This woman had a curse in her family, that was circling her and looking for a legal opportunity to land and afflict her. She had actually confessed, professed and done everything she knew to do, to keep this away from her and her family for years.

When she and her husband opened the door to this curse through their dishonor and thievery, the curse now had a legal reason to be able to land on her. Micah 2:1-3 shows what happened in this situation.

> Woe to those who devise iniquity,
> And work out evil on their beds!
> At morning light they practice it,
> Because it is in the power of their hand.
> They covet fields and take them by violence,
> Also houses, and seize them.
> So they oppress a man and his house,
> A man and his inheritance.
> Therefore thus says the Lord:
> "Behold, against this family I am devising disaster,
> From which you cannot remove your necks;
> Nor shall you walk haughtily,
> For this is an evil time (Micah 2:1-3).

God says that if someone who has been granted power through trust, uses that power to steal away inheritances, a disaster can come upon them that they won't be able to escape. This is what happened to this lady and her family. As a result of her participation in these deviant practices, the devil had a legal right to afflict her with a family curse. The devil was legally allowed to take her life even though God's passion was to heal her. The only way that the Lord could have healed her was if she had repented of that which she had done. Then the power of the curse would have been broken and God as Judge could have fulfilled His passion as Father, legally.

Remember, God cannot compromise Himself as Judge to fulfill His fatherly passion. We must grant Him the legal right as Judge to satisfy the desires of His heart as Father. Otherwise the devil wins and God loses, even though His passion is always to do us good. When we grasp this principle, we will stop asking, "Why didn't God do something?" whenever something bad happens. God cannot intervene until we give Him the legal right to do so. His passion is always to bless, heal and show mercy. This is why James 1:16-17 tells us that it is God's passion always to do good.

> Do not be deceived, my beloved brethren. Every good gift and every perfect gift is from above, and comes down from the Father of lights, with whom there is no variation or shadow of turning (James 1:16-17).

When we read in Scripture that something evil was done 'by God', my own personal opinion is that God did not 'do' it, he simply had to 'allow' it legally. When the devil has a legal right to perform evil, God must allow it unless someone comes to the court of Heaven to contest that right.

Let us look at the example of Job. God did not kill Job's children, afflict him with sickness or take away his wealth. Satan did. God did not want this to happen, but Satan presented a case showing his legal right to afflict Job. His accusations against Job concerned the motives of Job's heart. Job 1:9-11 we see Satan telling the Lord that Job was only serving God because God had blessed and secured him so much.

> So Satan answered the LORD and said, "Does Job fear God for nothing? Have You not made a hedge around him, around his household, and around all that he has on every side? You have blessed the work of his hands, and his possessions have increased in the land. But now, stretch out Your hand and touch all that he has, and he will surely curse You to Your face!" (Job 1:9-11)

It appears that everything is judged and evaluated in Heaven. Even when we are doing everything right, the devil can still question our motives. This is what threw Job into his tribulation. This tells me that we need to allow the Holy Spirit to, not only empower us to walk rightly, but also from a pure and clean heart. God had to allow these afflictions until Job set things in order and rescinded Satan's legal rights. Once Job did this, God rendered a judgment that restored to Job twice what he had lost.

When evil occurs, we should always look for the legal right that allows it. When we do, we can confidently go into the court of Heaven, deal with the legalities and shut the door on evil.

This principle explains why intercessors so often feel the passion of God in their prayer and yet nothing seems to change. It is very possible to feel what God feels, experience His desires and be unable to move anything in the spirit realm. Knowing God's heart and being able to administrate it legally are two very different things. If we want to see God's passion manifest on Earth, we must get things legally in place. The devil always resists God and us with legalities. The Lord will not override His own judicial system to grant His passion. He cannot. We must step into that system and grant Him the legal right to fulfill His passion.

Repentance – The Missing Key

In Matthew 16:18-19 Jesus said that the governmental people, His Ecclesia, that He would build, would use keys of authority to set in place legal things and remove legal things so His Kingdom purposes would be done.

> And I also say to you that you are Peter, and on this rock I will build My church, and the gates of Hades shall not prevail against it. And I will give you the keys of the kingdom of Heaven, and whatever you bind on earth will be bound in Heaven, and whatever you loose on earth will be loosed in Heaven." (Matthew 16:18-19)

The Church or Ecclesia has been given keys to bind and loose. As I shared in a previous chapter, the words bind and loose are legal in their nature. We, as God's individual and corporate people, are to go into the courts of Heaven and put binding things in place so God can legally fulfill His Father's passion. We are also to loose or dissolve contracts that the devil has in the Earth realm that allow him the legal right to kill, steal and destroy. He has to have a legal right to do it, our job is to remove that legal right from him. We do this through repentance for ourselves and our history and the history of our nations. Anything that the devil is doing in the nations is because our sins and the sins of our generations have granted him the legal right to do it. When we repent, we are removing his legal right of operation. We are breaking the devil's snare. 2 Timothy 2:25-26 tells us we break the snare and set people free through repentance.

> ... in humility correcting those who are in opposition, if God perhaps will grant them repentance, so that they may know the truth, and that they may come to their senses and escape the snare of the devil, having been taken captive by him to do his will (2 Timothy 2:25-26).

Notice that God grants repentance. Repentance is a legal activity that affects the courts of Heaven. When I repent and come into agreement with the testimony of the blood and the other voices, the accuser is silenced. The snare he has fashioned is broken, and we can escape. We are no longer bound to him to do his will, but are freed from his oppression. He no longer has a legal right to torment and terrorize us. When we repent, we grant God, as the Judge of all the legal right to render verdicts from His throne in agreement with His Kingdom purpose.

The Judge of all is waiting on us to give Him the legal right to manifest His goodness.

The Mandate of the Ecclesia

Genesis 18:20-21 shows us that God Himself went down to Sodom and Gomorrah to examine the cries and evidence before Him that demanded judgment.

> And the Lord said, "Because the outcry against Sodom and Gomorrah is great, and because their sin is very grave, I will go down now and see whether they have done altogether according to the outcry against it that has come to Me; and if not, I will

know" (Genesis 18:20-21).

Somehow or other the outcry against Sodom and Gomorrah had reached the throne of God. This cry was presenting evidence that the city was worthy of judgment and destruction. The Lord went down to investigate and validate the evidence that had been given. The Lord does something very interesting. He brings Abraham into the equation. Genesis 18:17-18 shows that God shares with Abraham what is about to happen.

> And the Lord said, "Shall I hide from Abraham what I am doing, since Abraham shall surely become a great and mighty nation, and all the nations of the earth shall be blessed in him? (Genesis 18:17-18)

A casual reading would cause us to think that God is just sharing information with Abraham because he is His friend. This is true, but there is a much deeper reason why God shared this with Abraham. He brought Abraham into the equation because God was seeking a legal reason to show mercy. He knew that Abraham would seek to give God a legal reason to show mercy. Genesis 18:22-26 shows that Abraham is seeking to give God a legal reason to spare this wicked place.

> Then the men turned away from there and went toward Sodom, but Abraham still stood before the Lord. And Abraham came near and said, "Would You also destroy the righteous with the wicked? Suppose there were fifty righteous within the city; would You also destroy the place and not spare it for the fifty righteous that were in it? Far be it from You to do such a thing as this, to slay the righteous with

the wicked, so that the righteous should be as the wicked; far be it from You! Shall not the Judge of all the earth do right?" So the Lord said, "If I find in Sodom fifty righteous within the city, then I will spare all the place for their sakes" (Genesis 18:22-26).

Please notice that Abraham petitioned God on the basis of Him being Judge and judging righteously. God agreed with Abraham and said He would not destroy it for the sake of fifty righteous. Abraham continued to petition God as judge and finally had it reduced to ten righteous men. The Lord said for the sake of ten righteous men He would spare the city and territory. Genesis 18:32-33 shows this legal exchange taking place.

Then he said, "Let not the Lord be angry, and I will speak but once more: Suppose ten should be found there?" And He said, "I will not destroy it for the sake of ten." So the Lord went His way as soon as He had finished speaking with Abraham; and Abraham returned to his place (Genesis 18:32-33).

God was looking for a reason to be merciful and knew that Abraham would endeavor to give it to Him legally. I have heard many people say that Abraham stopped too soon in his intercession. This is simply not true. In the culture of that day and in Jewish culture, ten denotes the smallest number that constitutes a government. God said that if He could find ten righteous men, the smallest number that could represent government, for the sake of those ten He would spare the city. We sometimes think we need the whole of population to repent, or at least the majority, to receive God's mercy. All we actually need is a governmental representation of the population to petition the courts of Heaven for mercy instead of judgment.

This is the job of the Ecclesia. To be that governmental representation who can operate in the court of Heaven to secure blessings from Heaven for a nation and a generation. God will spare nations for the sake of the Ecclesia within it, if we are righteous and carry recognizable, governmental authority in the courts of Heaven. God is looking for a reason to be righteous and show mercy. It is our job as His people to get things legally in place so as Judge He can fulfill His fatherly passion.

The Lord is Judge of all. He is also our Father who desires to bless us and release to us our inheritance. May we become proficient in His courts so He legally has the right as Judge to bless our going out and coming in. This is the passion of the Father's heart.

10

The Testimony of the General Assembly

When a judge enters a courtroom, it is customary that all rise in honor of the judge. There is to be an atmosphere of honor in the courtroom toward the judge and all the happenings of the court. The court holds within its power the ability to pass judgments that can alter lives with its decisions. So it is in the court of Heaven. If a natural, earthly court, has this power, how much more the Heavenly court where the Judge of All is presiding. In the court of Heaven, there is to be an atmosphere of worship and reverence in which all proceedings and verdicts occur.

This is why Scripture says that in this court of Heaven we have come to the General Assembly. Hebrews 12:23 says this.

> To the general assembly and church of the firstborn who are registered in Heaven, to God the Judge of all, to the spirits of just men made perfect (Hebrews 12:23).

The term General Assembly means universal companionship or a mass-meeting. This speaks of the multitude that is worshipping about the throne of Heaven from every tribe, tongue, nation and people. Revelation 7:9-12 gives us a glimpse of this mass-meeting of worship about the throne.

> After these things I looked, and behold, a great multitude which no one could number, of all nations, tribes, peoples, and tongues, standing before the throne and before the Lamb, clothed with white robes, with palm branches in their hands, and crying out with a loud voice, saying,
> "Salvation belongs to our God who sits on the throne, and to the Lamb!"
> All the angels stood around the throne and the elders and the four living creatures, and fell on their faces before the throne and worshipped God, saying:
> "Amen! Blessing and glory and wisdom, Thanksgiving and honor and power and might, Be to our God forever and ever.
> Amen" (Revelation 7:9-12).

In the court system of Heaven around the throne there is worship. Worship is a part of the proceedings of the court. Worship at its core is governmental in nature. Worship, in fact, creates the atmosphere that the Court of Heaven operates from. When we worship we take our place in the General Assembly that is in the court system of Heaven. Even though our feet are on the planet, in the spirit we ascend and become part of this worshipping multitude in the courts of Heaven. We often say that God's presence 'came', as we worshipped. I would like to present another concept. Perhaps the presence of the Lord didn't so much 'come' as we 'ascended' or 'went' into the atmosphere of the Throne and the courts of Heaven. When we worship, we step into the governmental process of the throne room of Heaven. We take our place in the throne room and from there become a part of the process of Heaven in rendering verdicts that touch and change the Earth. From our worship we shouldn't just get goose-bumps and a little teary-eyed. When our worship is joined to Heaven, we will exercise governmental authority out of the courts of Heaven. We can see this somewhat in Revelation 5:8-14. These verses show us that worship starts around the throne and moves from sphere to sphere until all of creation is worshipping.

> Now when He had taken the scroll, the four living creatures and the twenty-four elders fell down before the Lamb, each having a harp, and golden bowls full of incense, which are the prayers of the saints. And they sang a new song, saying:
> "You are worthy to take the scroll, And to open its seals;
> For You were slain,
> And have redeemed us to God by Your blood Out of every tribe and tongue and people and nation,
> And have made us kings and priests to our God; And we shall reign on the earth."
> Then I looked, and I heard the voice of many angels around the throne, the living creatures, and the elders; and the number of them was ten thousand times ten thousand, and thousands of thousands, saying with a loud voice:
> "Worthy is the Lamb who was slain
> To receive power and riches and wisdom,
> And strength and honor and glory and blessing!"
> And every creature which is in Heaven and on the earth and under the earth and such as are in the sea, and all that are in them, I heard saying:

> "Blessing and honor and glory and power
> Be to Him who sits on the throne,
> And to the Lamb, forever and ever!"
>
> Then the four living creatures said, "Amen!" And the twenty-four elders fell down and worshipped Him who lives forever and ever (Revelation 5:8-14).

Worship begins about the Throne with the four living creatures and the multitude of angels and elders - thousands times ten thousands of them. Then it invades every creature in Heaven, on Earth and under the Earth. It impacts those who are in the sea. They were all heard to be worshipping the Lord who sits on the throne. The worship that had its origin with the four living creatures about the Throne touches and involves all the creation of God before it is finished.

This tells me a couple of things. Worship doesn't originate on Earth, it originates in Heaven. The worship that God desires and is necessary to Heavenly judicial activity has, as its source, Heaven itself. The second thing this tells me is we are to become a part of the worship about the Throne and not be separate in our worship here in the Earth.

As we worship we are to enter and stand in the courts of Heaven helping to create the atmosphere from which judicial activity takes place. When we experience His presence in the Earth realm, it is because we have stepped into the realm of Heaven and have become a part of the process. This is why we see in Hebrews 12:22-24 that we have come to certain things. These things haven't come to us, we have come to them. We have moved into the spiritual dimension in Heaven. Though we may be in the natural realm in the Earth, simultaneously we can be in the spirit about the Throne of God in Heaven. This occurs through our interacting with the worship of Heaven and becoming a functional part of the General Assembly or mass-meeting about the throne.

The Tabernacle of David

We see this in the life of David and his establishment of Zion. One of the first things David did when he came to the full rulership of Israel was to establish the place called Zion. He retrieved the Ark of the Covenant from where it had resided and brought it to Jerusalem. He set up what became known as the Tabernacle of David on Mount Zion.

> So they brought the ark of the Lord, and set it in its place in the midst of the tabernacle that David had erected for it. Then David offered burnt offerings and peace offerings before the Lord (2 Samuel 6:17).

David cultivated and hosted the presence of God on Mount Zion. He established 24-hour worship there so he could effectively govern a nation from the presence of the Lord. The worship of David's tabernacle connected to the worship of Heaven allowing a flow of judicial activity from Heaven to Earth. David did not rule from natural abilities but from supernatural abilities out of Heaven.

If we are to function in the courts of Heaven effectively we must become worshippers. Our worship must be connected and joined to what is happening around the Throne of God. This is why Jesus said God is seeking worshippers. John 4:23-24 shows us the passion of the Father for worshippers to take their place.

> But the hour is coming, and now is, when the true
> worshippers will worship the Father in spirit and
> truth; for the Father is seeking such to worship Him.
> God is Spirit, and those who worship Him must
> worship in spirit and truth (John 4:23-24).

Notice that the Lord is not seeking worship but worshippers. When we worship in spirit and in truth, we qualify to function as God's governmental people. True worship enables us to step into the judicial process of Heaven with great reverence, fear, awe and honor. When we cultivate the heart of a worshipper, we will create an atmosphere in the Earth that can join with Heaven and see verdicts rendered out of the court system.

A story that helps relate this principle concerning worship happened to me after the Lord gave me a dream. In the dream I was shown that 9/11 occurred because of judicial activity in the courts of Heaven. The principalities and powers were granted the legal right to attack America because there was no Ecclesia or governmental people recognized in Heaven at that time to stop it.

As I awoke from the dream I had a distinct sense that if we didn't take our place in the courts of Heaven that another significant attack on American soil was coming. I called together the Ecclesia I apostolically led and shared that, for whatever reason, we had been assigned to stop any potential attack. We met as God's governmental people on 11/11/11. As we began to enter the courts of Heaven, I clearly sensed that we were in for a struggle. In fact, as we began to seek to deal with any legal issue that would allow another attack, I was aware of very strong demonic resistance. I actually wanted to back away and not pursue it any further, but knew I was in too deep. I was past the point of no return.

As the seer/prophet gifts were telling me what they were seeing and sensing, I was doing my best to get it in place in the courts. As the apostle in the matter, I was responsible for administrating what the seers/prophets were seeing and understanding. We were repenting of everything that was empowering the demonic hierarchy in its efforts to bring more destruction to America. Yet as we were doing this, nothing seemed to be changing. It appeared that the principalities had a case and we weren't getting things arranged for God's will to be done.

After quite a long period of time, I suddenly felt very strongly that we were to worship as we were in the courts, with a particular song. I began to lead the song acappella. As we worshipped with this song, I suddenly felt the atmosphere change. The seers/prophets confirmed that we had in fact got a rendering from the courts and had stopped another attack from occurring. I knew it because of the shift in that atmosphere that took place and the seer/prophets confirmed it by what they were seeing.

We had silenced the accuser and gotten a judgment of mercy from the Throne of Heaven over America. Mercy for America had been secured in whatever the issue was that Heaven needed us to intervene in. This happened because of our worship. Somehow our worship created an atmosphere and released testimony in the courts that granted God the Judge the legal right to fulfill His Father's passion.

Our worship creates atmospheres for the court to operate in, but also releases testimony into the courts that allows the Lord the legal right to implement His passion into the Earth. Worship is a very powerful tool in the courts of Heaven. We must be worshippers who declare His glory, kindness, passion, worthiness and holiness. When we do, our voice as the Ecclesia begins to agree with the other voices in the courts of Heaven.

Together we grant the Lord the legal rights to impact the Earth with His will and desire.

It is interesting that after this operation in the courts, the arrest of three terrorist suspects happened. A man named Jose Pimentel was arrested on November 20, 2011, for plans to bomb different places in New York City. On January 7, 2012, Sami Osmakac was arrested for his terrorist plot. In February 2012, Aminie El Khalifi was arrested for the plan he had devised to attack America as well. Whether these were directly related to our operation in the courts of Heaven cannot be proved beyond doubt. But I know that what was done through our operation and worship in the courts of Heaven put some things legally in place for God's will to be done. Our operations in the courts of Heaven are not only necessary for our personal and family lives, but also for nations. The Holy Spirit will guide us through this function to get the necessary legal things in place for the Father's will to be done.

There is no way that any of us would dare to enter a natural court in Earth and not honor the judge on his seat while seeking a favorable verdict from him. We intuitively know that honor is demanded and expected. As we seek to enter the courts of Heaven and see decisions and verdicts rendered on our behalf, may we increasingly become worshippers that please the heart of the Father. May we be a part of the worship of the One Who sits on the Throne Who creates atmospheres for judicial activity. From this atmosphere we are allowing God as Judge of all legally to be able to fulfill His fatherly passion. When this happens Heaven legally invades the Earth and His will is done here as it is in Heaven. What a privilege we have been granted. May all glory, honor, praise and thanksgiving be granted to Him Who sits on the throne.

11

The Testimony of the Ecclesia/Church

Anyone who speaks and gives testimony in a court must first be recognized. Everyone from the judge to the attorneys to the jurors to the witnesses must have been commissioned, assigned, authorized and sworn in. Judges are appointed to their bench by governmental leaders. Attorneys must be recognized by the court for the function they perform. Jurors are chosen and sworn in, as are witnesses who give testimony in the courts. If we are going to have impact in a court setting we must have jurisdiction to operate there. It is the same in the courts of Heaven. We are told that the Church of the firstborn is registered in Heaven for operation in the courts of the Lord. In other words we, as the Church/Ecclesia, have been granted a voice in the court system of Heaven. Hebrews 12:23 shows us this.

> To the general assembly and church of the firstborn who are registered in Heaven, to God the Judge of all, to the spirits of just men made perfect (Hebrews 12:23).

We, as the Church of the firstborn, have been registered in the courts of Heaven and therefore have been granted a jurisdiction in the courts. We have a legal right to operate in this court and are a part of the process of Heaven. This is so important and cannot be underestimated.

Knowing Your Jurisdiction

The Apostle Paul spoke of measurement of rule or the sphere he had been granted. 2 Corinthians 10:13 tells us that Paul stayed within his measurement, spheres, limits and jurisdiction.

> We, however, will not boast beyond measure, but within the limits of the sphere which God appointed us—a sphere which especially includes you (2 Corinthians 10:13).

If we are to be effective and protected, we must stay within the sphere that has been granted to us by God. The word in the Greek for sphere is metron. It means a measure or a limited portion. We each have been granted a metron to function in. When we function in that metron or limited portion appointed to us, we have success and protection.

As I mentioned in another chapter, there are varying levels of court operations in Heaven. Just as there are criminal courts, small claim courts, civil courts and other expressions in Earth, so in Heaven there are different dimensions of courts. We have to be recognized and registered to operate within a sphere of Heaven. To get outside our God ordained sphere is unproductive and very dangerous. We open ourselves to satanic onslaught, attack and even destruction.

The good news is that we can all operate in the court that the Bible calls the throne of grace. Every one of us as believers has rights, privileges and authorities in this sphere. Hebrews 4:16 tell us we are to come boldly to this court of Heaven.

> Let us therefore come boldly to the throne of grace,
> that we may obtain mercy and find grace to help in
> time of need (Hebrews 4:16).

We can come and present our petitions that relate to family and personal issues in this court. It is very easy to get verdicts rendered on our behalf in this court of Heaven. From His throne of grace the Lord will bless us with mercy and grace for our time of need. When we move past that which is personal and family oriented and step into intercession for churches, cities, states, regions and nations, we are entering a conflict which requires another jurisdiction. We must be recognized in Heaven to function in the courts of Heaven concerning these things. It is one thing to pray prayers of blessings over governments, rulers and territories; it is another thing to engage principalities that rule these places. In the courts of Heaven only those who have been granted jurisdiction should engage principalities and ruling powers. Contending with principalities that have been empowered through multiple generations of sin, is a very deadly and dangerous thing to do, if we are not recognized in the courts of Heaven on this level.

This is why the Bible speaks of the *Church* registered in *Heaven*. The Ecclesia/Church is God's legislative, governmental and judicial people and they have been registered and authorized to operate within the court system of Heaven. When the Church is functioning where it is meant to, we have an authority to get verdicts from the court against powers of darkness. With these verdicts in hand, we win on the battlefield every time. The issue is we must have the jurisdiction to accomplish these things. We cannot fake the spirit realm out. If we haven't been given the jurisdiction from Heaven to operate there, the spirit realm and its forces know it and will exploit it. We are no threat to them if we do not have legitimate authority.

In fact, if we do not carry realms of authority that the spirit dimension recognizes we can be in trouble. We see this in the occasion of the sons of Sceva in Acts 19:13-17. These begin to seek to use the Name of Jesus as a formula for exorcism without the authority associated with it.

> Then some of the itinerant Jewish exorcists took it upon themselves to call the name of the Lord Jesus over those who had evil spirits, saying, "We exorcise you by the Jesus whom Paul preaches." Also there were seven sons of Sceva, a Jewish chief priest, who did so. And the evil spirit answered and said, "Jesus I know, and Paul I know; but who are you?" Then the man in whom the evil spirit was leaped on them, overpowered them, and prevailed against them, so that they fled out of that house naked and wounded. This became known both to all Jews and Greeks dwelling in Ephesus; and fear fell on them all, and the name of the Lord Jesus was magnified (Acts 19:13-17).

These guys got themselves in trouble because they tried to engage the demonic without carrying jurisdiction in the spirit realm to do it. The result was chaotic and treacherous. We cannot fake the spirit realm out. They know whether we have the authority we are seeking to function in, or if we do not. It is imperative that we carry authority and jurisdiction before we seek to uproot and remove powers of darkness.

Apostolic Jurisdiction

The key to an Ecclesia and its jurisdiction is the apostle to which it is joined. Apostles carry the governmental authority that causes an Ecclesia to arise. Every true Ecclesia recognized in Heaven is connected and joined to apostles. 1 Corinthians 12:28 says the Lord has set the apostles first.

> And God has appointed these in the Church: first apostles, second prophets, third teachers, after that miracles, then gifts of healings, helps, administrations, varieties of tongues (1 Corinthians 12:28).

When Jesus builds an Ecclesia He begins with an apostle. 1 Corinthians 12:28 shows us the order and ranking of the Lord and His government.

> And God has appointed these in the Church: first apostles, second prophets, third teachers, after that miracles, then gifts of healings, helps, administrations, varieties of tongues (1 Corinthians 12:28).

The Lord has set the apostle first. The word "first" is the Greek word "proton" and it means first in rank, importance, preeminence and influence. In other words when the Lord begins something, He starts with an apostle. This is why Jesus spent 3½ years calling and fashioning apostles. On the Day of Pentecost in the upper room, the apostle along with the other 120, were empowered with the Holy Spirit. The Church then "came out of the apostles" not the "apostles out of the Church."

This is still the divine order of God today. When God gets ready to raise a governmental people recognized in heaven, He begins it with an apostle.

The apostle is first in prominence, authority, and influence. He then joins to that apostle, a people that will carry and function in governmental and judicial authority in the courts of Heaven. Different Ecclesias carry different jurisdictions. The jurisdiction of an Ecclesia is determined by the jurisdiction of the apostle who birthed it and the apostles who are joined to it.

Apostles have varying realms of authority and jurisdiction. Paul spoke of not being less than the greatest of apostles. 2 Corinthians 11:5 speaks to this understanding.

> For I consider that I am not at all inferior to the most eminent apostles (2 Corinthians 11:5).

The fact that Paul spoke of great apostles says that there are apostles with different rankings in the spirit realm. Just like there are one star generals all the way up to five star generals in the United States of America military, there are also different levels of authority among apostles. Some apostles have jurisdiction over a small town. Other apostles have jurisdiction in major cities. Still other apostles have jurisdiction in States or territories. God even has apostles that have jurisdiction in nations. The jurisdiction of an apostle will determine the jurisdiction of the Ecclesia which he or she leads.

That Ecclesia can then go with the apostle into the courts of Heaven and be a part of getting verdicts out of Heaven granting God the legal right to fulfill His passion as Father in the Earth. This is a critical key to seeing society changed and nations being discipled. To reclaim society back to a Kingdom culture, it will require the legal reason the devil has resisted us to be removed.

Once these legal reasons of resistance are removed we can then implement Kingdom influence back into our culture.

To help understand these ideas let me share with you a personal story. As a result of some very severe backlash against me, I am very careful about how I operate in determining my God ordained jurisdiction. Backlash from the devil occurs for two reasons. One reason is that we do not have authority to do what we are trying to do. We are outside our jurisdiction. We have believed our own press reports and not sought the Lord to determine our true measurement of rule.

The other reason for backlash is where we are within our jurisdiction, but there is something in our history that gives the devil a legal right to attack us. We must learn how to set our personal history in order so that when we step into our jurisdiction, the devil has no legal right to attack us. We do this through repentance. Any personal sin issues in my history or bloodline must be thoroughly repented of and brought under the blood of Jesus. Without this, demonic powers have a legal right to attack us as we seek a legal footing against them.

As I was learning (and continue to learn), how to operate in the courts of Heaven, I invited a ministry from South Africa into Colorado Springs where I lived. They were the first ministry I saw functioning in the courts of Heaven. This ministry is led by Natasha Grbich, who is a seasoned intercessor and apostolic leader. Her words to me as I began to teach on the courts of Heaven were, "You have given us language for what we have been doing for twenty years." I had witnessed how they operated and had recognized a strategy from the Lord that we as the Church knew little about. I know it is a missing key and strategy that will take us as the Church into the next dimension.

As this ministry came into Colorado Springs to be with me for some meetings, the Lord spoke to me before they were to arrive and said, "Declare that Natasha and her team have a right to be in this city because you invited them."

I didn't know how significant this would be. At one of the services, we were in the courts of Heaven seeking judgments and verdicts from the Throne when suddenly a principality came into the court of Heaven and asked Natasha, "Who said you could be here?" This interaction in the court was witnessed by one of the seer prophets that functions with Natasha. This seer prophet then went on to relay how the principality continued asking questions, "Did Steve Bach say you could be here?" and "Did Hickenlooper give you permission to be in this State?"

Here is the amazing thing about this, Bach was the Mayor of Colorado Springs and Hickenlooper was the Governor of Colorado at this time. This little seer prophet from Africa had no way of knowing this naturally, but heard the powers of darkness asking the questions. The powers of darkness wanted to know, "Who, in authority, gave Natasha the right to be in this region of the world and be taking us to court?" These principalities were seeking to resist our function in the courts of Heaven by questioning if Natasha was outside her jurisdiction as a South African.

Natasha looked at me and said, "You must come and answer this." So I stepped forward and said, "I, Robert Henderson as an apostolic leader residing in Colorado Springs, invited and have allowed these to be here." Suddenly I knew why God prompted me to make that declaration a few days before they arrived. The principalities seek to use the issue of jurisdiction to resist us from accomplishing things in the court system of Heaven. The powers of darkness will always question our measurement of rule in the court. They know what your measurement is, but do you?

They now knew that Natasha and the team had a legal right

to be in our city and function there because of my invitation. However, the wrangling did not stop there. The powers of darkness that were seeking to diminish and take away our legal jurisdiction then asked of me, "Who are you?" Again, this was being revealed by what the seer prophet was seeing happening in the spirit realm. Obviously it was a natural progression in the wrestling that was going on in the court system of Heaven. If I was the one who had invited Natasha into the city, then the question was, "Who was I?"

Let me say that these powers knew who I was. They wanted to see, did I know who I was. I began to answer before the court of Heaven that I was an apostle sent by the Lord Jesus Christ to the city of Colorado Springs. After several moments before the courts of Heaven it was established by the courts that I had a jurisdiction in the courts of Heaven and had a right to bring Natasha and the team into the city to function there.

All of this was about who had the right and measurement of rule to function in the courts of Heaven concerning Colorado Springs. The powers of darkness will use the issue of jurisdiction to resist and disqualify us from operating in the courts of Heaven. We have to be well established and our realms of authority must be documented in the courts of Heaven for us to operate there. We must be registered in Heaven for the realms in which we are seeking to operate.

Again, we can speak blessings over anything. But if we are going to wrestle with principalities in high places for regions of the Earth we must have a recognized jurisdiction in that realm. Apostles, and the Ecclesias they lead, must be registered in Heaven. We should also know that what the Earth applauds, many times Heaven doesn't recognize. Just because someone has a reputation in Earth does not mean they have a jurisdiction in the spirit realm. Again, we cannot fake the spirit realm out.

Here is one more story that helps us understand being registered in Heaven. During the summer of 2012 a very strong wild fire broke out in Colorado Springs. It made international news for several days as the firefighters battled to bring the blaze under control. It was later stated that this fire moved at three football fields per second, destroying 347 homes as it came into the Colorado Springs city limits.

Two months before this fire erupted, one of my sons had a prophetic dream. In his dream he saw Pikes Peak, which is the mountain Colorado Springs is under, spewing out fire like a volcano. The main point of his dream was that while homes were burning all around us, our home had a shield of protection from God around it that would not allow it to burn. This is exactly what happened. The fire raged around us and neighborhoods very close to us were destroyed, while our home and neighborhood were divinely protected. The fire was so close to our home that we were evacuated for five days.

The day after we were evacuated the television reported that the same weather conditions that had driven the fire to consume all these homes would continue and that more of the city was in danger. The fire was only 5% contained and was still burning out of control. There was much trepidation in the city as everything possible was being done to control the fire.

As all this was going on, I heard the Lord say, "You have the authority to stop this fire." I knew He meant that we could go into the courts of Heaven and break what was driving this fire. There are always wild fires in Colorado during the summer, but somehow or other this fire was now being driven by the consuming powers of the devil. When the Lord said, "I had the authority to stop it", I knew this was a part of my jurisdiction. Because I am an apostle and lived in Colorado Springs, this granted me authority in the courts of Heaven to deal with this destroying fire.

I called together a total of ten people that operate in a seer gifting to help me discern what was happening in the spirit realm. As we began to pray and submit ourselves to the Lord, the spirit realm opened up to the seers with me. Whatever dimension of jurisdiction an apostle carries, seer and prophetic gifts will begin to see into that dimension. An apostle's authority will open that realm in the spirit arena. The gifts that are functioning connected to that apostles' call will begin to "see" what is happening in the unseen world.

As I began to pray with these seers, they began to sense and see what was driving this fire. They immediately saw a dragon with his claws in the ground. This dragon, which clearly was a ruling force in the spirit realm over Colorado Springs said, "This is mine because they gave it to me." In other words I have the right to consume this territory with fire and destruction because someone from the past gave this territory to me.

The seers then sensed and saw two things. Somewhere in the history of the region children had been offered in fire. This was the sin of Molech. Molech was a god of the Ammonites that people honored by causing their children to be burned as offerings. (Leviticus 18:21) They would offer their seed as a sacrifice to this demonic god. This most likely occurred when native groups ruled the land. The burning of children in sacrifice to demonic gods and the spilling of blood was empowering this dragon legally to consume the region.

The seers also saw General Palmer repenting for whatever his sins were in the courts of Heaven. The Bible says there is a great cloud of witnesses that are surrounding us and about the Throne of Heaven. We have talked about this in previous chapters. We agreed with Palmer's repentance and also repented for anything General Palmer had done that would allow this fire the legal right to burn. This was our realm of jurisdiction. General Palmer was one of the chief founders of Colorado Springs and was a godly man from all accounts. But founding fathers' sins can have a great effect when devils are looking for legal rights to reign and control.

We repented as the Ecclesia of God in the region and took away the legal right of this dragon to consume the land. We sensed clearly that things were shifting and verdicts were coming from the court of Heaven in our favor and in favor of the region. The seers actually saw the dragon's claws come out of the ground and the dragon leave the court. We had taken away the legal right of the principality to consume and destroy.

Once this was done, I then apostolically began to proclaim and decree that the weather patterns change. The forecast was for low humidity, high winds and dry thunderstorms to drive the fire the next five days. I began to decree high humidity, moisture in the air and everything that made it conducive for the firefighters to extinguish the flames.

This is exactly what happened. Every day the news would forecast unfavorable conditions and every day, they were wrong. The weather changed and favored the firefighters! In a matter of days the fire was 100% contained and no longer posed a danger to the city.

I firmly believe this was because we took away the legal right of the devil in the court of Heaven to consume the land. Once this was done we were free, as a representation of the Ecclesia, to make decrees from the courts of Heaven that Heaven backed up. There were many people praying that helped in this matter, but I also know that things shifted because of strategic activity in the courts of Heaven. An Ecclesia, registered and recognized in Heaven's courts, used their authority to grant God the legal right to spare and bless a region. We must walk in the jurisdiction that Heaven grants us.

The Lampstand

There is one final thing that I want to point out concerning the Church that is recognized and registered in Heaven. Jesus spoke to the Church of Ephesus and warned them that if they didn't repent, they could lose their lamp stand. This is found in Revelation 2:4-5.

> Nevertheless I have this against you, that you have left your first love. Remember therefore from where you have fallen; repent and do the first works, or else I will come to you quickly and remove your lampstand from its place—unless you repent (Revelation 2:4-5).

When Jesus threatened to remove the lampstand, He was warning that this church would lose its governmental authority and its right to function in the courts of Heaven. The lampstand spoke about the Church's identity and jurisdiction. To understand this we need to examine the meaning of a lampstand. In Zechariah 4:1-6 we see the prophet having a vision of two olive trees fueling seven lamps.

> Now the angel who talked with me came back and wakened me, as a man who is wakened out of his sleep. And he said to me, "What do you see?"
> So I said, "I am looking, and there is a lampstand of solid gold with a bowl on top of it, and on the stand seven lamps with seven pipes to the seven lamps. Two olive trees are by it, one at the right of

the bowl and the other at its left." So I answered and spoke to the angel who talked with me, saying, "What are these, my lord?"

Then the angel who talked with me answered and said to me, "Do you not know what these are?"

And I said, "No, my lord." So he answered and said to me:

"This is the word of the Lord to Zerubbabel: 'Not by might nor by power, but by My Spirit,' Says the Lord of hosts (Zechariah 4:1-6).

These two olive trees, fuelling the seven lamps with perpetual oil, speak of the anointing that empowers the Church. I want to focus in on the source of this anointing which is said to be these two olive trees. Revelation 11:3-6 tells us that these two trees carry certain DNA.

And I will give power to my two witnesses, and they will prophesy one thousand two hundred and sixty days, clothed in sackcloth." These are the two olive trees and the two lampstands standing before the God of the earth. And if anyone wants to harm them, fire proceeds from their mouth and devours their enemies. And if anyone wants to harm them, he must be killed in this manner. These have power to shut Heaven, so that no rain falls in the days of their prophecy; and they have power over waters to turn them to blood, and to strike the earth with all plagues, as often as they desire (Revelation 11:3-6).

These two witnesses that are the two olive trees feeding the lamps are of the nature and DNA of Moses and Elijah. Moses turned water to blood and struck Egypt with plaques while Elijah shut the Heavens and did not allow it to rain. The purpose of both of these prophets was to affect nations. Moses delivered a nation through his ministry while Elijah turned a nation back to God. They each carried governmental anointing and authority.

This is to be the anointing and authority flowing out of the olive trees and feeding the lamp stand of the Church. When Jesus says He is going to remove the lampstand, He is threatening to remove their recognized place in Heaven. If this were to happen, they would still be deemed a church on Earth but not recognized in Heaven.

This is the case of many groups today. They may be called churches on Earth but they are not Ecclesias as far as Heaven is concerned. They are not registered in Heaven. They have either lost their jurisdiction or never had it. We must have Ecclesias that are recognized in Heaven if we are to function there and see verdicts come out of Heaven.

We are looking for true apostles to birth real Ecclesias that Heaven recognizes. When this happens we have the right to take our place and see Earth changed as a result of the verdicts of Heaven.

12

The Voice of Angels in the Court

Evidence is a very important element in any court case. Judgments are rendered on the basis of the evidence presented in court. A judge may know that a decision should go a certain way, but if there is no evidence given to warrant that decision, the judge cannot render it.

A dear Korean friend of mine that translates in a court system of a large American city told me a story that accented this point. It seems that a young lawyer was trying to present a case before a judge. He was having a difficult time in getting everything communicated properly. The judge in the situation actually stopped the young attorney and said, "Young man, I can see what you are trying to do, but you are going to have to help me here". In other words the judge in the situation wanted to render a verdict in favor of the case the young attorney represented, but could not until the evidence was properly presented. So it is in the courts of Heaven. The righteous Judge of All must have proper legal reasons presented to Him for righteous verdicts to come forth.

In the court of Heaven, angels have the important task of gathering and presenting evidence. They release the necessary testimonies and evidence needed for God to render judgments.

A husband and wife I know were involved in a wrongful

death suit. One of their daughters had died in a traffic accident and they believed that a trucking company was at fault. The evidence presented in the lawsuit confirmed that the trucking company was indeed at fault and the judge rendered a verdict in their favor. At the conclusion of the trial, the judge approached this couple and expressed his sympathy for their loss. As a father, he empathized with the pain of their situation and wanted to help them. As a judge, there was nothing he could do until the evidence was presented and he could legally render a judgment. The evidence warranted the judgment that the jury delivered and it was very evident that the judge was pleased with the verdict. His years of judicial activity in our court systems caused him to rejoice when justice was done.

The Judge of all also needs evidence presented that warrants the verdicts He desires. This is why I say, it is our job to agree with the voices of Heaven and present our case until we grant God, as Judge, the legal right to fulfill His fatherly passion.

All the voices in Heaven operate for this purpose, but it is our job to agree with them until legal precedents are in place. God will never just render a judgment; He needs the input and agreement from the Church on Earth because man has been given this authority in the Earth realm. Psalm 115:16 says that the children of men have the God ordained authority in the Earth.

> The Heaven, even the Heavens, are the Lord's; But the earth He has given to the children of men (Psalm 115:16).

The Lord will not normally overstep the authority He has granted us. If we, as humans, are in authority in the Earth realm, then it is up to us to grant God the legal right to accomplish His will here. We must know how to exercise this authority in the courts of Heaven to give God the legal right to intervene on Earth.

Angels are a huge part of this process. Hebrews 12:22 declares that there is an innumerable company of angels that is a part of the court system of Heaven. The term innumerable company in the Greek actually means a ten thousand, myriad and indefinite number. The word *angels* means *a messenger and one who brings tidings*. There are innumerable angels in the courts of Heaven that all have different jobs. Some are there to worship, some are there to declare and decree and some are there to run with messages.

There are at least four ranks of angels operating within the court system of Heaven. I have heard teaching that says there are ten ranks, but for our purpose we will deal with four. Colossians 1:16 names the thrones, dominion, principalities and powers as dimensions of ranks.

> For by Him all things were created that are in Heaven and that are on earth, visible and invisible, whether thrones or dominions or principalities or powers. All things were created through Him and for Him (Colossians 1:16).

People normally think of this as depicting a satanic hierarchy structure. This is, however, a structure in the spirit realm that operates in the satanic realm, but also in the Heavenly realm. Satan is not a creator. Any structure that he uses was copied from what he had seen in Heaven. He was a part of the hierarchy structure of Heaven and knows it well. This structure was first, and still is, the structure of Heaven. Notice that all these things were created through Him and for Him. All these ranks were created to assist this Lord in fulfilling his agenda. Let us look at these ranks of angels in an attempt to understand some of the operations of this innumerable company.

Thrones

The first rank mentioned is thrones. This word in the Greek means to sit, a stately seat, a potentate. Anyone who sits on a throne in Heaven has a voice in the Heavenly court. Remember that there are thrones around The Throne in Heaven. (Daniel 7:9) Scripture records that there are 24 thrones around God's Throne, but there are probably many more. I would suggest that archangels are some who sit on these thrones. The word *archangels* come from the Greek word *archo* and means first in rank and political power. If thrones are listed first in the spirit realm this means they must be occupied by archangels. 1 Thessalonians 4:16 says that archangels will accompany Jesus at His return.

> For the Lord Himself will descend from Heaven with a shout, with the voice of an archangel, and with the trumpet of God. And the dead in Christ will rise first (1 Thessalonians 4:16).

The voice of an archangel has the power to bring dead people back to life. Archangels are very powerful beings. Michael is also said to be an archangel. Jude 8:9 tells us that Michael contended with the devil.

> Likewise also these dreamers defile the flesh, reject authority, and speak evil of dignitaries. Yet Michael the archangel, in contending with the devil, when he

disputed about the body of Moses, dared not bring against him a reviling accusation, but said, "The Lord rebuke you!" (Jude 8-9)

Michael as an archangel was very careful to stay within his jurisdiction. He actually invoked the Lord Himself to rebuke the devil. If Michael, one of the archangels of Heaven, is so careful to stay within his jurisdiction, how much more should we? Also please be aware that in John 5:28-29 Jesus said that this voice would indeed bring people in the graves back to life.

Do not marvel at this; for the hour is coming in which all who are in the graves will hear His voice and come forth—those who have done good, to the resurrection of life, and those who have done evil, to the resurrection of condemnation (John 5:28-29).

It states here that it is Jesus' voice that will bring them from the grave and yet when Jesus comes back, it is with the voice of the archangel. If it is in fact the voice of the archangel speaking on behalf of Jesus, it is as if Jesus Himself is uttering the words. Suffice it to say that these archangels carry great power and authority from the Lord. They, therefore, from the position of thrones have influence in the courts of the Lord.

Dominions

The next rank of angel mentioned is dominions. In my opinion, the angels known as cherubim are in this rank. Exodus 25:21-22 states there are two cherubs over the mercy seat that cover the ark of the covenant.

> You shall put the mercy seat on top of the ark, and in the ark you shall put the Testimony that I will give you. And there I will meet with you, and I will speak with you from above the mercy seat, from between the two cherubim which are on the ark of the Testimony, about everything which I will give you in commandment to the children of Israel (Exodus 25:21-22).

Moses was taken to Heaven and given a 'tour' of, among other things, the Tabernacle. Then God commanded him to make a replica on Earth of what he had seen in Heaven. The above Scripture shows that he was instructed to place two cherubim (a type of angel) over the mercy seat, just as it is in Heaven.

From this place, God said, He would meet with Moses and speak with him from the mercy seat. I am glad that the voice of the Lord always flows from His mercy. When we hear the Lord's voice, it is from the mercy seat of Heaven. Hearing His voice is part of the privilege of being in the courts of the Lord. The real ark of the covenant is actually in the court system of Heaven. The Apostle John saw this ark and the real mercy seat. Revelation 11:19 reflects and demonstrates what he saw.

> Then the temple of God was opened in Heaven, and the ark of His covenant was seen in His temple. And there were lightnings, noises, thunderings, an earthquake, and great hail (Revelation 11:19).

There are two cherubim who stand over the real ark and cover it with their wings. Scripture teaches that, prior to his being cast out of Heaven, Satan was a covering cherub Ezekiel 28:14 declares this.

"You were the anointed cherub who covers;
I established you;
You were on the holy mountain of God;
You walked back and forth in the midst of fiery
stones" (Ezekiel 28:14).

There are three things revealed about cherubs here. The first thing is they are anointed. They have a supernatural empowerment to fulfill their function. Secondly, they cover and defend. This is why the two cherubim are seen with their wings over the mercy seat. They guard the presence and mercy of the Lord. The third thing mentioned is that they are on the holy mountain of God. A mountain always speaks of government. This holy mountain's name is Zion. It is the place of government and the court system of Heaven. We have come to this place. (Hebrews 12: 22).

Cherubim have a function in the courts of Heaven to help verdicts come forth that fulfill the Father's passion. We choose to agree with the function of this rank of angels even when we don't fully understand. We, by faith, agree with the order of Heaven to see God's will be done on the Earth.

Principalities

The third rank of angels mentioned is principalities. When we hear this word we normally think of demonic powers. There are demonic principalities, but they originally were principalities in God's order and Kingdom. The demonic principalities fell with Lucifer before time began. They were cast out of Heaven for their rebellion against God. They then ceased to be angelic powers in the Heavenly realm and became demonic entities against the will of God. Principalities were probably seraphim when in Heaven. Isaiah 6:1-3 shows us one of the functions of the seraphim.

> In the year that King Uzziah died, I saw the Lord
> sitting on a throne, high and lifted up, and the train of
> His robe filled the temple. Above it stood seraphim;
> each one had six wings: with two he covered his
> face, with two he covered his feet, and with two he
> flew. And one cried to another and said:
> "Holy, holy, holy is the Lord of hosts; The whole
> earth is full of His glory!"
> (Isaiah 6:1-3)

The seraphim declare perpetually the holiness of the Lord.
This same scenario that Isaiah saw, the Apostle John saw and
recorded in Revelation 4:8.

> The four living creatures, each having six wings,
> were full of eyes around and within.
> And they do not rest day or night, saying:
> "Holy, holy, holy, Lord God Almighty,
> Who was and is and is to come!" (Revelation 4:8)

The previous verses say that these living creatures had the face
of a lion, a calf, a man and a flying eagle. I believe it is possible
that Isaiah recorded things that John later added to. These were
seraphim that are creatures before the throne and are declaring
the holiness of God in Heaven's courts. The interesting thing
about this is that the term seraphim actually means a flying
serpent. We tend to think that serpents are always evil, yet they
had their origin in the courts of Heaven. Remember that the
serpent in the Garden of Eden was sentenced by God to crawl
on its belly after it yielded itself as Satan's vehicle to deceive

Eve. Prior to this, it was probably a flying creature. This is what made the judgment of God against the serpent so strong. God again, cast Satan down from his exalted place and made him crawl on his belly in the dust.

Principalities of the demonic sort that now influence regions of the Earth are many times seen as dragons. These are fallen seraphim that have chosen to align with Satan in his transgression against the Lord. I have had several dreams, which have helped me understand this better.

After our move to Colorado Springs, I was told by the Lord in a dream, that I had been assigned to the city and the demonic principalities knew it. The result, in this dream, was lightning bolts being thrown at me by these principalities.

As time progressed I had another dream. In this dream I was under a church structure in the city. I was seeking to clean up things that were polluted and defiled in the unseen realms of this church. As I was reaching into a dark, cavernous place I suddenly disrupted and disturbed a creature. When this creature emerged from this dark place, it was a serpent with a dragon's head on it. It stood about 30 feet tall and was very intimidating. I knew it was the prince that influenced the region.

This serpent with a dragon's head was a fallen seraphim that had been assigned by demonic hierarchy to this region of our nation. It was a seraphim that used to fly, but had now lost its glory and was set against the purposes of God. I share this simply to make the point that seraphim are flying serpents with six wings. They function in the courts of Heaven. The fallen seraphim are now principalities that function within regions to resist the will of God.

To underscore the significance of this, let me share one more dream that brought me great understanding. I had a dream where a well-known apostle's wife sent me his response to the

9/11 attacks on the USA. 9/11 was when America was attacked and the twin towers in New York City fell. The world changed forever on that day. In the dream I received his documented response on a piece of paper with a letterhead. At the bottom of the page, there was a handwritten note from his wife. She had noted what she had seen prior to 9/11 in the court system of Heaven that allowed this tragedy to occur. In the courts of Heaven, the four living creatures were crying out, "Holy, Holy, Holy is the Lord God Almighty." They were releasing their testimony before the courts of Heaven. However, there were also their demonic counterparts in the courts of Heaven. These demonic principalities were declaring before the courts of Heaven, "BOC denied, BOC denied, BOC denied."

In my dream, I knew that as a result of these words, destruction had hit America. When I awoke I tried to figure out the significance of "BOC." I Googled this word and discovered that it is an acronym for Body of Christ. I understood immediately that the Lord was showing me how the enemy had a legal right to withstand the Body of Christ in the courts of Heaven.

The devil had found a legal right to resist the Body of Christ and its influence in the courts and perpetrate the 9/11 attacks. It wasn't God's will or God's judgment on America. It was a failure for us, as the Body of Christ, to take our place as the Ecclesia and grant God the legal right to thwart the plans of the devil. Because we have not understood this, we are still suffering the consequences of 9/11 until this day.

The demonic powers had a legal right to deny the Body of Christ the necessary influence we should have had in the courts of Heaven. They were therefore able to do the will of Satan rather than the will of God. We must learn how to come into agreement with the voice of the seraphim that cries out, "Holy, Holy, Holy" rather than empower the demonic principalities that are looking for a legal right to destroy. Nations and their destinies hang in the balance. It is our job as the Ecclesia to grant God the legal right to show mercy rather than allow destruction.

Powers

The final rank of angels is powers. This word means jurisdiction or authority. Psalm 103:20 mentions angels as part of the hierarchy of Heaven.

> Bless the Lord, you His angels,
> Who excel in strength, who do His word,
> Heeding the voice of His word (Psalm 103:20).

The word angel here means to dispatch as a deputy. This makes sense since they are the ones who do His word. These are the angels that carry out the verdicts that come from the courts of the Lord. They come to empower us and help us execute any and every judgment from the courts of Heaven.

There are many functions of these angelic beings. One of them is to land scrolls that carry judgment of the Lord against anything that is standing in the way of God's Kingdom purpose. We see this in Zechariah 5:1-4.

> Then I turned and raised my eyes, and saw there a flying scroll.
> And he said to me, "What do you see?"
> So I answered, "I see a flying scroll. Its length is twenty cubits and its width ten cubits."
> Then he said to me, "This is the curse that goes out over the face of the whole earth: 'Every thief shall be expelled,' according to this side of the scroll;

and, 'Every perjurer shall be expelled,' according to that side of it."

"I will send out the curse," says the Lord of hosts; "It shall enter the house of the thief

And the house of the one who swears falsely by My name.

It shall remain in the midst of his house And consume it, with its timber and stones" (Zechariah 5:1-4).

Zechariah was a prophet who prophesied during the restoration period of Israel. There were many enemies to this restoration process. Clearly there were thieves and perjurers that were stealing away the assets necessary for restoration. Suddenly, the prophet encounters an angel that is revealing a scroll that carries judgment against these thieves and perjurers.

Judgments or verdicts against what is resisting God's will come from Heaven's court as scrolls in the spirit realm. They are scrolls or judgments that must be landed and made manifest on Earth.

We are in a process of restoration, just like they were in the days of Zechariah. Acts 3:19-21 shows us that everything the prophets spoke of must be restored before Jesus can return.

Repent therefore and be converted, that your sins may be blotted out, so that times of refreshing may come from the presence of the Lord, and that He may send Jesus Christ, who was preached to you before, whom heaven must receive until the times of restoration of all things, which God has spoken by the mouth of all His holy prophets since the world began (Acts 3:19-21).

There is actually a four-step process revealed here. It begins with our *repentance*. The next phase is God's response to our repentance with *refreshing*. Then from refreshing we move to restoration. Then from restoration comes the *return*.

Notice that Heaven is holding Jesus until the restoration of everything that the prophets spoke of becomes a reality in the Church and the world. The knowledge of the glory of the Lord will cover the Earth as the waters cover the sea. (Habakkuk 2: 14).

We have watched the Lord send moves of refreshings as the body of Christ has repented. Part of this was the Toronto Outpouring and the Revival at Pensacola. But now it is time for Restoration to flow out of the refreshings. The restoration is a recovering of apostolic power and authority that sets the Church into a new dimension of operation. As this occurs, the Earth will experience a new level of Kingdom power being administrated and experienced. The devil is resisting this restoration on a corporate and even personal level. We need scrolls/books released from the Heavenly courts to remove every hindrance holding back restoration. The Ecclesia has two jobs. The first is to get verdicts from the courts of Heaven. The second job of the Ecclesia is to land these verdicts/scrolls until everything functionally that is standing in the way of restoration is removed.

I use the word landed, because, just as an airplane needs to find a landing strip in order to land on Earth and release its cargo, so it is with scrolls. Scrolls/Books are Heavenly instructions that should produce a tangible result in the Earth realm. Just like an airplane, they need to find a landing strip where they can touch Earth and release the verdict so that the will of Heaven can be done on Earth.

Zechariah sees the scroll as a result of an angel showing it to him. When he sees it, he can read it, receive the instruction and carry it out on Earth. I am convinced that our prayers and activities in the court of Heaven have resulted in many scrolls/ books being released. The problem is we haven't seen them to land them. This has hindered Kingdom order coming into the planet.

The job of the Ecclesia is to grant God the legal right to fulfill His Kingdom passion. Once this is granted, we must land the scrolls/verdicts/judgments that come from the courts of Heaven. This requires angelic help. We need the angelic powers that have been deputized from Heaven to open our eyes and help us land the scrolls. Until these scrolls/books from Heaven are landed that which is standing in the way of God's will being done, will continue to resist. We need angelic and prophetic help to be able to move out of the way all that is resisting God's will from being done.

May the Lord open our eyes to the angelic powers that operate out of the courts of Heaven. I am convinced that much has already been released and simply needs to be landed. Once this occurs we will see Kingdom order and justice come to the Earth. Nations will shift and come into Kingdom destiny because we as the Ecclesia are accomplishing our mandates from Heaven. We are granting God the legal right to fulfill His passions and then with angelic help we are landing His righteous judgments in the Earth. "Come Your Kingdom, be done Your will, on Earth as it is in Heaven!"

13

The Testimony of the Bride

Without exception, Mary, my wife of 35 plus years, has the greatest influence over me. We have been together since we were 16 years old and in High School. That history alone grants her great influence in my life. Add to this, my profound respect for her wisdom and prophetic gifting and I pay very close attention to her and what she thinks.

Why am I sharing this? The next voice that gives testimony in the courts of Heaven is listed as the city of the living God, Heavenly Jerusalem. It doesn't take a great Bible scholar to realize this term refers to the Lamb's wife. Revelation 21:9-10 shows us the connection between this city and the bride of the Lord.

> Then one of the seven angels who had the seven bowls filled with the seven last plagues came to me and talked with me, saying, "Come, I will show you the bride, the Lamb's wife." And he carried me away in the Spirit to a great and high mountain, and showed me the great city, the holy Jerusalem, descending out of Heaven from God (Revelation 21:9- 10).

John is taken to a high mountain, which I believe is Mount Zion. The angel wants John to see the Bride from the place of governmental and judicial activity. He doesn't want John to simply see the Bride as the lover of the Lord, but rather as the governmental entity that brings Heaven into Earth.

Much has been written about this city, but to me, it is a clear depiction of Heaven invading Earth. It is a picture of a Heavenly influence that can be invoked over natural cities until they reflect the glory of God and His Kingdom culture. The Bride's voice and testimony give God the legal right to invade Earth. The Bride is the lover of the Lord and her voice has great impact in the courts of Heaven.

One of the best places we see the power of a bride influencing the verdicts of Judges, Kings and Potentates is in the life and relationship of David and Bathsheba. David had promised that the child of his union with Bathsheba, Solomon, would be King by the mandates of the Lord. However, when David was weak and close to death, another son tried to arise and take the throne. Bathsheba went to David at the urging of the prophet Nathan and made an appeal to the king. Remember now, appeals happen in courtrooms. The result of the appeal is that David calls Bathsheba to him to declare that Solomon will be king. Her appeal as the Bride was heard. 1 Kings 1:28-31 records this.

> Then King David answered and said, "Call Bathsheba to me." So she came into the king's presence and stood before the king. And the king took an oath and said, "As the Lord lives, who has redeemed my life from every distress, just as I swore to you by the Lord God of Israel, saying, 'Assuredly Solomon your son shall be king after me, and he shall sit on my throne in my place,' so I certainly will do this day." Then Bathsheba bowed with her face to the

earth, and paid homage to the king, and said, "Let my lord King David live forever!" (1 Kings 1:28-31).

King David made a judgment and rendered a verdict based on the appeal of Bathsheba. Her history as his lover and wife gave her an influence that resulted in this judgment.

We must realize that when we are the Lord's bride and have a history of loving and worshipping Him, we have great influence in the courts of Heaven. For our sake the Lord will render judgments that allow Heaven to invade Earth. The Bride of Christ within any city can get verdicts out of Heaven that allow reformation of the city. Charles Finney made a profound statement that resonates to this day. He said, "Revival is no more a miracle than a crop of wheat. Any city can obtain revival from Heaven when valiant souls enter the conflict determined to win or die or if necessary to win and die."

This statement says to me that when we as the Bride of Christ position ourselves in prayer in the courts of Heaven, we grant God the legal right to invade the Earth. The result will be Heaven's influence coming to Earth until cities reflect His glory and Kingdom culture.

God is Doing a New Thing
Isaiah 43:18-20 shows what God will do for the sake of His people and the aftermath of that.

"Do not remember the former things,
Nor consider the things of old.
Behold, I will do a new thing,
Now it shall spring forth;

Shall you not know it?
I will even make a road in the wilderness
And rivers in the desert.
The beast of the field will honor Me,
The jackals and the ostriches,
Because I give waters in the wilderness
And rivers in the desert,
To give drink to My people, My chosen
(Isaiah 43:18-20).

The Lord promises a new thing that will be done. Notice that He says He will do it. The question is, will we know it and recognize it when it happens? It seems unfathomable, yet it is quite possible for the Lord to do something new and we, His people, completely miss it and stay stuck in the old. We must ask the Lord to make us sensitive and aware of His new thing so we don't persecute and dismiss the new thing of the Lord.

The Lord promises to bring rivers in the desert and roads in the wilderness. **He** will do this for the purpose of giving His people drink. He does this for His chosen. And notice that when He does this, even the animals will be affected. Scripture says that the beasts will honor Him. This means that when God responds to His Chosen people, even unredeemed people and societies will be affected, reformed and transformed. My point is, it all begins out of the love of the Bridegroom for His Bride. He will do for the Bride what would not otherwise be done. The result will be rivers flowing in the desert, Heaven invading Earth.

The Authority of the Bride

We have to realize the authority and influence we have in Heaven as the Bride. Song of Solomon 4:9 shows the passion that erupts in the heart of Jesus toward His bride.

> You have ravished my heart, My sister, my spouse;
> You have ravished my heart With one look of your
> eyes, With one link of your necklace
> (Song of Solomon 4:9).

The Bridegroom wants the Bride to understand the effect she has on Him. His heart becomes ravished and greatly moved with passion when she looks at Him. When we worship, yearn and long for the Lord, His heart is moved. In these moments of intimacy great things can be asked for and received. The term *pillow talk* is used sometimes to express the secrets and longings exchanged between two lovers. During times of intimacy hearts are unlocked and things are expressed that would not be expressed at other times.

In a sense we can have pillow talk with the Lord. During times of intimate exchange we can ask for things and see the Lord respond because we have ravished His heart. We can actually inaugurate activity in the courtroom from the bedroom of intimacy with the Lord. From this place of great influence we can see cities saved and Heaven touch Earth.

When the Heavenly city begins to invade natural cities through the Bride's governmental and judicial administration, we will see real transformation in our cities. Kingdom culture will develop within the city as the Heavenly city becomes superimposed upon it. Let us examine some of the changes one can expect when the Heavenly city descends to Earth.

The Government of God Over Cities

Natural cities can begin to have the government of God operating within it that will result in peace and tranquility coming to that city. There will also be prosperity and blessing wherever the government of God is established. The city of the living God is Heavenly Jerusalem. Jerusalem always speaks of the government of God. Jerusalem is the seat from which the Lord would govern the Earth. Jeremiah 3:17 shows that Jerusalem is the Throne of God.

> At that time Jerusalem shall be called The Throne of the Lord, and all the nations shall be gathered to it, to the name of the Lord, to Jerusalem. No more shall they follow the dictates of their evil hearts (Jeremiah 3:17).

The reason there has always been such a battle for natural Jerusalem is because it is destined to be the seat of God's government. This is why it was attacked and even destroyed. This is why when people were sent back to restore it, there was always contention. In Ezra 4:16, King Artaxerxes was cautioned that if he allowed Jerusalem to be rebuilt that he would have no more dominion within that region.

> We inform the king that if this city is rebuilt and its walls are completed, the result will be that you will have no dominion beyond the River (Ezra 4:16).

When we get Heavenly Jerusalem out of Heaven and over cities in the Earth, these cities begin to take on governmental qualities. The government of God invades the Earth. Not only does that city experience the blessings of living under God's Kingdom rule, but from that city, Kingdom rule can go forth. This is the result of the Bride loving the Bridegroom and seeing verdicts come from Heaven because of her influence.

The Beauty of the Bride in Our Cities

Another thing that happens as a result of the Bride's influence in Heaven is that the beauty of the Lord is seen within natural cities. Revelation 21:2 shows this affect of Heaven invading Earth.

> Then I, John, saw the holy city, New Jerusalem,
> coming down out of Heaven from God, prepared as
> a bride adorned for her husband (Revelation 21:2).

The beauty of the Bride prepared for her husband will begin to determine what a city looks like. As the Bride becomes more and more prepared for her husband, the Lord, she begins to dictate the atmosphere of a city. Right now principalities and powers of the demonic realm are determining what cities look like. As the Bride is prepared, she will win judgments in the court of Heaven that will dethrone these demonic powers and take the seat of dominion in the spirit realm from which they once ruled. When this occurs the beauty of the Bride of Christ will create an atmosphere within cities where His splendor is known. The beauty, purity and holiness of the Bride will prevail in the atmospheres of cities.

Revelation 21:3 tells us that God will begin to dwell in the Earth realm as a result of the Bride and this city coming down.

And I heard a loud voice from Heaven saying, "Behold,

the tabernacle of God is with men, and He will dwell with them, and they shall be His people. God Himself will be with them and be their God" (Revelation 21:3).

Whole cities can become the dwelling place of God. If the Bride within a city can wield her influence in the courts of Heaven, that city can host the presence of the Lord. We talk about the presence of the Lord being in a service or among His people, what would happen if the presence of the Lord tabernacled in a city?

Everything would be blessed in that city. People would drive into that city and get saved. Is it possible for the Bride to be so influential in the courts of Heaven that the rule of principalities is broken and the presence of the Lord replaces it? I believe that it is not only possible, but it is our portion. We don't have to yell and scream at the devil, we simply take up our place as the Bride of Christ. Using our God-ordained influence in the courts, we can unlock what is in the books of Heaven about a city and see His Kingdom culture established.

Healing Our Cities

When Heaven invades Earth, wounds are healed and tears dry up. Revelation 21:4 says,

And God will wipe away every tear from their eyes; there shall be no more death, nor sorrow, nor crying. There shall be no more pain, for the former things have passed away" (Revelation 21:4).

Our cities can become a place of healing instead of a place of wounding. We see this in the book of Acts 8:6-8 where Philip preaches the Gospel of Kingdom rule and a whole city comes to joy.

> And the multitudes with one accord heeded the things spoken by Philip, hearing and seeing the miracles which he did. For unclean spirits, crying with a loud voice, came out of many who were possessed; and many who were paralyzed and lame were healed. And there was great joy in that city (Acts 8:6-8).

Great joy came to the city of Samaria because the rule of the Kingdom impacted and brought Heaven to Earth. There is so much pain, hatred, animosity and disillusionment in our cities today. Imagine what it will be like when the Bride takes her place in the courts and grants the Lord the legal right to establish Kingdom rule?

We see this in the days of Elisha when Jericho was a pleasant city but the waters in the city were poisoned. The prophet knew what to do to heal the waters so the pleasantness of the city could be restored. 2 Kings 2:19-22 shows that God healed the waters so there was no more barrenness.

> Then the men of the city said to Elisha, "Please notice, the situation of this city is pleasant, as my lord sees; but the water is bad, and the ground barren."
>
> And he said, "Bring me a new bowl, and put salt in it." So they brought it to him. Then he went out to the source of the water, and cast in the salt there, and said,
>
> "Thus says the Lord: 'I have healed this water; from it there shall be no more death or barrenness.'"
> So the water remains healed to this day, according to the word of Elisha which he spoke (2 Kings 2:19-22).

This happened right after Elijah was taken away and Elisha had received his mantle. It is interesting to me that the men came to Elisha and made their request. I am sure the water had been bad for a long time and, for whatever reason, the water had not been healed during Elijah's tenure. When the 'leadership' changed, they came to Elisha and asked him if he could solve the problem of the city. He took a new bowl and put salt in it. He then went to the source and poured the salt in the water and healed the waters. With that, healing came to the city.

Let me point out several things here. First of all Elisha asked for a new bowl. He, in fact, was the new bowl. He was in essence saying that what the old administration had not done, he, as the new administration, would do. He was making a distinction between the old and the new. He wasn't tearing down the old, he was establishing himself as the new. This is important. If we are to see cities healed we must accept the new administration that God is establishing. Elisha would carry the mantle in a different way than Elijah did and would bring healing to cities.

Secondly, he placed salt in the bowl. We are the salt of the Earth as the body of Christ. We are to be the answer for cities that are crying out for healing.

And thirdly, they went to the source. The source of the problem is what is ruling the cities. The principalities and powers that rule our cities must be summoned to and legislated against in the court of Heaven. Yelling, screaming and cursing will not get the job done. We must have verdicts from the courts that remove these powers and allow us as the salt of the Earth to take our place.

Having followed this protocol, Elisha's proclamation could then bring lasting results. The waters stayed healed. When we establish legal precedents, our decrees settle affairs permanently. This is the job of the Bride within a city. Our influence as the Bride of Christ gives God the legal right for Heaven to invade Earth. Cities can be healed and God's Kingdom culture established. May the Lord grant us the wisdom, understanding and enlightenment to function as His Bride, agree with the other voices of testimony and see cities reformed for the glory of God.

14

The Testimony of Finances

During my tenure of leading an apostolic center in Texas, a lady came to me after one of the services and put a sum of money in my hand. She told me that she was sowing this for her alcoholic husband who had been on a drinking binge and was now in a rehabilitation centre. The doctors had told her that the damage of this last binge was permanent and he would never be the same. In fact he could be incapacitated for the rest of his life. They actually used the term, 'a vegetable'.

At the time that she gave me the money, I did not understand what she was doing. I am not sure she understood except that the Lord had told her she was to sow this money for her husband's restoration. Two days later, the Lord told me to go to the rehabilitation center and pray for this man. I contacted the lady and arranged to travel to the center with her. When we walked into the room, the gentleman was slouched in a wheelchair with drool dribbling out of his mouth. He seemed completely unaware of our presence.

I knelt in front of him, put my hands on his knees and prayed a very simple prayer for complete restoration. To my amazement, this man began to revive. In a few short minutes he and his wife were dancing the Texas Two step right in front of me! It was absolutely one of the most significant miracles I have ever witnessed, simply because of the way it happened.

It would be many years before I understood at least some of

the spiritual things that occurred to produce this miracle. This man was completely delivered, healed, restored and spent the remainder of his days in complete service to the Lord. He had spent the major part of his life as an alcoholic, but from that day he never drank again because of what Jesus did for him. The courts rendered a verdict of healing for him because of the testimony of the finances his wife sowed.

Finances have a Voice

Your finances and money have a voice that is heard in the courts of Heaven. When we sow we are not just supporting a worthy cause or ministry. When we sow, we are releasing and amplifying our voice in the courts of Heaven. Hebrews 7:8 declares a very powerful truth.

> Here mortal men receive tithes, but there he receives them, of whom it is witnessed that he lives (Hebrews 7:8).

This Scripture is speaking of our tithes and offerings. We are not bringing them to a Levitical priesthood. We are bringing them to Jesus, our High Priest who belongs to the eternal priesthood of Melchizedek. There in this Scripture speaks of the courts of Heaven where Jesus functions as our High Priest. When we bring these offerings to the Lord, it produces a witness in the courts of Heaven. The word witness means one who gives judicial testimony. Our money has a testimony in the courts of Heaven. It speaks in the court system of God on our behalf.

Raising a Memorial

Our money carries our faith and all that is in our heart and speaks when we sow it into the Kingdom of God. This is what happened to Cornelius in Acts 10:3-4. His prayer mingled with his offerings and created a memorial before the Lord.

> About the ninth hour of the day he saw clearly in a vision an angel of God coming in and saying to him, "Cornelius!"
>
> And when he observed him, he was afraid, and said, "What is it, lord?"
>
> So he said to him, "Your prayers and your alms have come up for a memorial before God (Acts 10:3-4).

We know the result of this was the Gospel entering the Gentile world through this man's house. His diligent seeking of the Lord and his giving created this memorial before the throne of God that resulted in an angelic visitation.

The word memorial simply means a reminder or to bring to memory. This is what happens at memorials. We remember. Memorials speak to us about our heritage, intent, sacrifice and even a sense of responsibility to continue what someone else started. The monuments in our nation are designed to speak to us and cause us to remember what it cost for our nation to exist. These memorials speak to elicit from us actions consistent with the sacrifices of our forefathers.

Every year, in the South where I grew up, my family would go to the country cemetery where portions of our family were buried. The first Saturday of June each year, the whole family would gather at this cemetery. There would be an interdenominational service where we sang and someone brought a message. Afterwards, we would have lunch under the pavilion that had been specially built for these events.

In its heyday, there were hundreds of people at these gatherings. People would drive for several hours to spend the day with family and friends. People who had grown up in that community (or their parents/grandparents had been raised there) would bring their children and show them off for all to see. It was a tradition that I remember well. I would meet cousins I didn't even know I had. These gatherings were called memorials.

When we were adults, my mom would still ask us, "Are ya'll coming to the memorial." (Remember, I am from the South.) The answer to that question had better be, "Yes." She wanted her family to be a part of this tradition and memorial. I often wondered why this was called a memorial. I now understand it was because there was a need to remember. We needed to get together and allow our heritage to speak to us to remind of us of where we had come from and how we should not forget the values that had brought us this far.

When the angel said to Cornelius that his activities had come before God and created a memorial, he was saying it had caused God to remember him. A memorial is something that speaks and stirs memory and hopefully actions. Part of what stirred God to action was the sound and memorial that Cornelius's offering made in Heaven. It was releasing judicial testimony as a witness before the courts of Heaven.

There are a couple of places in the Old Testament where we see memorials being created so Heaven can respond based on testimony being released. In Numbers 5:26 we are told of the memorial portion of an offering and what the priest was to do with it.

And the priest shall take a handful of the offering, as its
memorial portion, burn it on the altar ... (Numbers 5:26).

When someone brought a certain offering prescribed by the
law, the priest would take a handful of the grain and burn it on
the altar. As the smoke from the altar and the offering ascended,
it carried with it the idea that Heaven received this portion and
it created a memorial before God. This is why it was called the
memorial portion. The rest of the offering was for the priest and
his livelihood. The memorial portion was intended to speak in
Heaven and cause God to remember the one who had brought
the offering. This offering had a voice that caused God to
remember.

Your Offering Has a Voice
Another place we see this is in Numbers 10:10. As the
people would bring their offerings, Aaron and his sons would
blow trumpets over the offering. The Bible says this created a
memorial before God.

> Also in the day of your gladness, in your appointed
> feasts, and at the beginning of your months, you
> shall blow the trumpets over your burnt offerings
> and over the sacrifices of your peace offerings; and
> they shall be a memorial for you before your God: I
> am the Lord your God" (Numbers 10:10).

The blowing of the trumpets over the offering caused a memorial
to be before God. It would release testimony in the courts of
Heaven that granted God legal right to answer the cry of our
hearts. Trumpets speak of the prophetic voice. In 1 Corinthians

14:8-9, Paul refers to the spiritual gift of prophecy as a trumpet that needs to give a clear sound.

> For if the trumpet makes an uncertain sound, who will prepare for battle? So likewise you, unless you utter by the tongue words easy to understand, how will it be known what is spoken? For you will be speaking into the air (1 Corinthians 14:8-9).

When we bring our offerings, we should sound the trumpet or prophesy over our offerings. Whatever we prophesy over our offerings is the sound and testimony they will carry into the courts of Heaven. On the basis of the voice of our offerings, God is free to render judgments and verdicts on our behalf.

We see this in the case of Abel's offering to God. In Hebrews 11:4, God testifies of Abel's offering.

> By faith Abel offered to God a more excellent sacrifice than Cain, through which he obtained witness that he was righteous, God testifying of his gifts; and through it he being dead still speaks (Hebrews 11:4).

Notice the wording. Abel obtained a *witness* that he was righteous because God was *testifying* of his gifts. The word witness means to give *evidence*. It comes from the word that means to witness *judicially*. The word testifying is the same Greek word, *martureo*. In both cases the Scripture is implying a courtroom setting. Abel obtained judicial testimony that he was righteous, because God bore witness and testified of his gifts. In other words, God as judge accepted the testimony of Abel's offerings and rendered Abel righteous. This verdict still stands today. Not only is his life still speaking as a testimony, but Abel won for himself a place of influence in the courts of Heaven because of his faithfulness and the testimony of his offerings. Our offerings have a voice in the courts of Heaven.

We see this played out in Deuteronomy 26:16-19. This whole chapter is about the commands God gave concerning offerings. He commanded the people to worship Him with their firstfruits and tithes after they came into the Promise Land. In the verses mentioned, the Lord shows what would happen as they kept the command to worship Him with their offerings.

This day the Lord your God commands you to observe these statutes and judgments; therefore you shall be careful to observe them with all your heart and with all your soul.

Today you have proclaimed the Lord to be your God, and that you will walk in His ways and keep His statutes, His commandments, and His judgments, and that you will obey His voice.

Also today the Lord has proclaimed you to be His special people, just as He promised you, that you should keep all His commandments,

and that He will set you high above all nations which He has made, in praise, in name, and in honor, and that you may be a holy people to the Lord your God, just as He has spoken" (Deuteronomy 26:16-19).

The Lord commands these ordinances to be kept on *this day*. Then He says that when they keep these ordinances today, they are *proclaiming* their commitment and loyalty to God. In other words, when they brought their offering and kept the command, their offering began to proclaim or testify before the Lord.

Notice the next verse says that on the basis of this testimony, God now proclaimed or rendered a verdict over them. He began to declare them blessed above all nations and that they were set on high. Our offerings have a voice and can create a testimony in Heaven when we know how to bring them.

We should know that our finances carry the present tense statement of our hearts into Heaven. Remember that the judge can only render verdicts based on the evidence presented. If we bring our offerings with uncleanness, bitterness or unforgiveness in our hearts, our offerings will give the 'wrong' testimony in Heaven's court. This is why Jesus in Matthew 5:23-24 says we are to deal with any estrangement before we bring our offering.

> Therefore if you bring your gift to the altar, and there remember that your brother has something against you, leave your gift there before the altar, and go your way. First be reconciled to your brother, and then come and offer your gift (Matthew 5:23-24).

If we bring an offering into the courts of Heaven with unforgiveness in our hearts, it releases the wrong testimony in the courts. We do not want the results of this testimony in our lives. Jesus actually goes on to say that if we bring these gifts while in this state, the court of Heaven can release verdicts that put us in prison. Matthew 5:25-26 chronicles this.

> Agree with your adversary quickly, while you are on the way with him, lest your adversary deliver you to the judge, the judge hand you over to the officer, and you be thrown into prison. Assuredly, I say to you, you will by no means get out of there till you have

paid the last penny (Matthew 5:25-26).

An offering offered with bitterness releases testimony in the courts of Heaven that gives our adversary the legal right to have us delivered to a prison. We must make sure that our offerings carry a good testimony. This is so very important. If our offerings brought with problems in our heart have this much power on the negative side, then how powerful it must be when done with right attitudes and motives.

We see this in Malachi 3:3-5. The prophet is prophesying about the coming of the Messiah and His purging effect. He is declaring that the purpose for this purging is so we can bring an offering in righteousness. Wow! Offerings must really be important to God's agenda being carried out if the Messiah's purpose for coming was to empower us to bring righteous offerings. These verses help us to understand this.

> He will sit as a refiner and a purifier of silver; He will purify the sons of Levi, And purge them as gold and silver, That they may offer to the LORD An offering in righteousness.
>
> "Then the offering of Judah and Jerusalem Will be pleasant to the LORD, As in the days of old, As in former years. And I will come near you for judgment; I will be a swift witness Against sorcerers, Against adulterers, Against perjurers, Against those who exploit wage earners and widows and orphans, And against those who turn away an alien—Because they do not fear Me," says the LORD of hosts (Malachi 3:3-5).

Notice that when we are purged, as priest (which is what the sons of Levi speak of), then we are able to present an offering in righteousness. When every wrong motive is purged and every attitude adjusted, then our offering will be accepted.

Notice that the result of offerings being received and accepted is that God begins to judge. Remember that judgment is courtroom activity. Based on what our offerings, presented in righteousness, are testifying, God begins to be a witness and release judgment against everything afflicting society and His purpose in society. Our offering presented with a pure heart after our purging, releases evidence in the courts of Heaven that allows God as Judge to deal with every destructive thing touching our society. He judges sorcery, adultery, perjurers, inequity, economic oppression and injustice against the needy and poor. When we, as the Ecclesia and people of God, bring our offerings with a right heart, we are releasing testimony against that which is working against society. How powerful is this? Our offerings don't just meet needs; they produce judicial sounds that gives God the right to fulfill His passion in the Earth. When we bring an offering in righteousness, we come into agreement with Heaven and give the Father legal right to render judgments on our behalf.

A Review of the Nine Voices

There are nine voices that are speaking in the courts of Heaven concerning the Lord's Kingdom desire and His passion for us as Father. In review, these nine voices are the blood, the Mediator, spirit of just men made perfect (great cloud of witnesses), The Judge, the general assembly, the Church of firstborn, the innumerable angels, the bride and our offerings.

We must learn to agree with the intercession of Heaven that

each brings and establish evidence that grants God the legal right as Judge to fulfill His fatherly passion toward us. This is our job as individuals before His throne of grace and as the Ecclesia. In the last chapter, I will seek to bring it all together and share how to bring cases before the Lord and His court.

15

Presenting Cases in the Courts of Heaven

Now that we a have better understanding of the courts of Heaven, let's learn to present our petitions and cases before the Lord. I want to seek to bring everything together so that at the conclusion, you can step into this dimension and see God's passion toward you fulfilled. The entire purpose for these final thoughts is to empower us to move with boldness and confidence before the Lord.

Get Off the Battlefield

The first thing we must do to step into the courts of Heaven is to get off the battlefield. We have to recognize the need for legal precedents to be set before we run to the battle. We are in a conflict, but it is a legal one. Remember that Jesus never pictures prayer in a battlefield context. He did put prayer however in a courtroom or judicial setting in Luke 18:1-8.

In this parable a widow is seeking a verdict of justice from an unrighteous judge. Among other things, one glaring aspect of this story stands out. This woman, in her efforts to deal with her adversary, never spoke to her adversary, but only to the judge. She understood that when a rendering could be obtained from the judge, then her adversary became of no consequence.

The adversary's legal footing for hurting, harming, stealing or otherwise tormenting her would be removed. The adversary would have to bend the knee to the verdict of the court. Once the court rendered a verdict then it could be executed into place. The verdict from the court is the legal wrestling, the executing it into place is the battlefield part. We have tried to run to the battlefield without verdicts from the court. We have found ourselves ineffective or even soundly defeated. Those days are over as we get off the battlefield and into the courtroom.

This is what the Apostle Paul was referring to in Ephesians 6:12.

> For we do not wrestle against flesh and blood, but against principalities, against powers, against the rulers of the darkness of this age, against spiritual hosts of wickedness in the Heavenly places (Ephesians 6:12).

The term wrestle is a very apt term for what goes on in the courts of the Lord. Through our maneuvering in the courts we actually put into place the legalities necessary for God's Kingdom will to be done. If you have ever been in a natural court setting you will attest to this. Attorneys maneuver, operate and wrestle with each other to get the legal upper hand. The same is true in the court of Heaven, especially when dealing with principalities over regions. It is our job to enforce the legal judgment that Jesus won at the cross, on the powers of darkness, stripping them of all illegitimate authority that they hold over us individually and corporately. It takes some legal wrangling to set this in place. Once it is done, we can then march onto the battlefield and win every time. The battle in the courtroom always precedes the victory on the battlefield. This whole book is about learning to win in the courtroom so we can win on the battlefield. Once we have had a change of perspective and see the primary place of conflict as a courtroom, we are ready to present our case.

Presenting Our Case

We can only present our case once we have read from the books in Heaven. Daniel 7:10 sets the scene.

> A fiery stream issued
> And came forth from before Him.
> A thousand thousands ministered to Him;
> Ten thousand times ten thousand stood before Him.
> The court was seated,
> And the books were opened (Daniel 7:10).

The good news is that the books are open. The books are not closed, locked, or sealed. This means we can discern and understand by revelation what is in the books. On a personal level, the books reveal our Kingdom purpose and destiny. This is not a once-off revelation, but rather an ongoing journey of discovery.

When we are dealing with cities, states, or nations, prophets will help us understand God's Kingdom will as it is written in the books. When a prophet prophesies, they are simply reading out of the books of Heaven. They are unveiling the secrets contained in the books.

Once this is done, apostles with jurisdiction in the given sphere can begin to present the case before the courts. We present the city, state, or nation in the court and remind the Lord of what He wrote about it in the books. We are presenting our case and putting God into remembrance. (Isaiah 43:26-27).

This operation sets the court in motion. Just as in a natural court, the proceedings start with the prosecution presenting its case. It is a powerful thought that we as mortal people have the authority to set in motion the courts of Heaven, but it is true.

When we present from the books what has been written before time began, court comes to session. This is why in Daniel 7, the court is seated, and the books are open. The court is going to make decisions based on what is presented from the books of Heaven by us as individuals and as the Ecclesia. It is an awesome place God has given us.

Agreeing with Our Accuser

Once we have presented the case for what has been written in the books, we will almost always encounter the accuser seeking to deny us what is in the books. (Revelation 12:10) Any and all accusations that he brings to seek to disqualify us from getting what is in the books must be answered. This will require us to repent and humble ourselves before the Lord for nations and ourselves.

It is interesting that right after the Lord speaks the parable in Luke 18:1-8, that His next teaching launches into two men who went up to pray. The one was a Pharisee and the other a tax collector. This parable is in Luke 18:9-14. Jesus contrasts how the Pharisee was self-righteous and very arrogant, while the tax collector was very humble and surrendered. The end of the parable was that the tax collector went down to his house "justified" rather than the religious Pharisee.

> Also He spoke this parable to some who trusted in
> themselves that they were righteous, and despised

others: "Two men went up to the temple to pray, one a Pharisee and the other a tax collector. The Pharisee stood and prayed thus with himself, 'God, I thank You that I am not like other men—extortioners, unjust, adulterers, or even as this tax collector. I fast twice a week; I give tithes of all that I possess.' And the tax collector, standing afar off, would not so much as raise his eyes to heaven, but beat his breast, saying, 'God, be merciful to me a sinner!' I tell you, this man went down to his house justified rather than the other; for everyone who exalts himself will be humbled, and he who humbles himself will be exalted" (Luke 18:9-14).

Jesus spoke this parable in connection to or as an extension of His teaching on praying from a judicial place. To be justified means to render as just or innocent. To be justified is a legal position of being found not guilty and innocent. One of the things Jesus is teaching in connection to operating in the courts of Heaven, is that God responds to humility and surrender. I have found that humility and surrender carry great weight in the courts of Heaven. If we want to have an audience in the courts, we must appear there with a humble spirit and a broken and contrite heart. These sacrifices, God will not despise. (Psalm 51:17)

Through repentance we set in place the voice of the blood of Jesus and every other voice releasing testimony. Remember that there are nine voices that can speak in the court system of Heaven. We can agree with these voices in several ways. One of the primary ways we can agree is through our repentance. When we sense accusations being used against us, we should simply agree with them. Matthew 5:25 says we are to agree with our adversary quickly.

> Agree with your adversary quickly, while you are on
> the way with him, lest your adversary deliver you to
> the judge, the judge hand you over to the officer, and
> you be thrown into prison (Matthew 5:25).

To agree with our adversary simply means that we are quick to repent of anything being used against us in the courts. I have no need to answer for myself. I don't justify myself. I allow the blood of Jesus to justify me. I also draw from any/or all of the other voices in the courts that would speak as well. They will speak on my behalf when I have repented and accessed the blood.

My attitude is that I can never go wrong with repentance. Self- justification can destroy me, but repentance will cause me to be accepted. My experience has been that as I repent for anything in my history or even bloodline issues, the Holy Spirit will grant me repentance. (2 Timothy 2:25). As I began to repent for things in my bloodline that I was not even aware of, it isn't uncommon for me to begin to feel real remorse. I have been moved to tears, as the Holy Spirit brought conviction and sorrow into my heart, so that my repentance was real. This took away the accusations of the devil and silenced his ability to disqualify me.

Confessing Our Sin

Our words before the throne of God are very powerful. In Hosea 14:1-2 the prophet is urging the people to use 'words' to return to the Lord.

O Israel, return to the Lord your God,
For you have stumbled because of your iniquity;
Take words with you,
And return to the Lord. Say to Him,
"Take away all iniquity; Receive us graciously,
For we will offer the sacrifices of our lips (Hosea
14:1-2).

Right words before the courts of the Lord are very powerful. Because of our words, God will forgive us. The sacrifices of our lips in departing from iniquity and returning to the Lord, give God the legal right to forgive us. This is why John told us to confess our sins. 1 John 1:9 declares that our confession, or saying what God says about something, grants the Lord legal right to forgive and cleanse us.

If we confess our sins, He is faithful and just to forgive us our sins and to cleanse us from all unrighteousness (1 John 1:9).

Our words set legal things in motion. Our words become testimony and agreements with the courts of Heaven. Our words grant the Lord the legal right to fulfill His passion toward us, which is always mercy and goodness. This is a part of what overcomes the accuser of the brethren, the word of our testimony. Revelation 12:10-11 declares that the word of our testimony in agreement with God's purposes overcomes and silences accusation.

Then I heard a loud voice saying in Heaven, "Now salvation, and strength, and the kingdom of our God, and the power of His Christ have come, for the

> accuser of our brethren, who accused them before our God day and night, has been cast down. And they overcame him by the blood of the Lamb and by the word of their testimony, and they did not love their lives to the death (Revelation 12:10-11).

Part of the word of our testimony is to 'confess' and use words to grant God the legal right to be merciful to us.

Another thing that allows us to come into concert and agreement with the voices of Heaven and silence the accuser is our offerings. As I shared in the previous chapter, our finances have a voice. When we bring finances with a clean heart and full of passion toward the Lord, these finances add a voice of agreement with Heaven. It is appropriate to offer finances and then prophesy over them and with them into the courts of Heaven. When we do, we are becoming a part of the operation of Heaven to see His will done on Earth.

Resisting the Devil

Once the accuser has been silenced and the wrestling match in the courts is finished, we are now set to rebuke any and all demonic forces. This may include the rebuking and renouncing of any and every demonic activity. It is amazing how quickly the operation of the devil is stopped and removed once his legal rights are thwarted. When we have put in place through our repentance the legalities of Heaven, the devil will have to stop and desist any and all operations. The legal right has been removed and the rights of his operation are broken. If we have rebuked the devil and it hasn't moved, it is because he still has a legal right to be there. Colossians 2:13-14 shows us that Jesus set in place every legal thing necessary to break satanic holds.

> And you, being dead in your trespasses and the uncircumcision of your flesh, He has made alive together with Him, having forgiven you all trespasses, having wiped out the handwriting of requirements that was against us, which was contrary to us. And He has taken it out of the way, having nailed it to the cross (Colossians 2:13-14).

Every bit of 'paperwork' against us in Heaven, Jesus nailed it to His cross and took it out of the way. The words handwriting of requirements actually means a legal document and/or a law, ordinance or decree. In other words, positionally Jesus dealt with every accusation or bit of 'paperwork' that the accuser can use to resist us in the courts of Heaven. It has been removed. This doesn't mean that the devil will not try to use it. Whether it is our sin or the sin of our bloodline. Just as we had to appropriate what Jesus did for us when we were born again (and it wasn't just automatic), there are times where, in specifics, we must appropriate or execute it into place. The devil will seek to use things against us. We must take the blood of Jesus and with our repentance and faith put what Jesus did for us in place in that given area. We verbally and with faith accept and forcibly put into place the work of Jesus on the cross in our behalf. When we do, we have taken away any legal footing the devil tries to use.

The word contrary in these verses means covertly. The sacrifice of Jesus deals with even the 'hidden' things in our bloodline that are standing against us. When, by the Spirit revelation, these bloodline issues come to light, we repent of these things, apply the blood of Jesus and break any place the devil might be trying to exploit. When we do, we become positioned to functionally get verdicts from the courts of Heaven. The accuser has been silenced and God is now free to answer our prayer from His Father's heart. Any legal place Satan has been using against us is taken away.

I have found that once the legal right is broken, he will go when he is resisted. James 4:7 is very clear.

> Therefore submit to God. Resist the devil and he
> will flee from you (James 4:7).

Submitting to God involves humility, surrender, repentance and submission to the Lord. Once this is in place and any and every place of rebellion is out of us, we will resist and he will flee. The devil no longer has a legal right to stay. Our rebuke now carries power and he will flee.

Making Decrees

The last thing we do as legal things have now been ordered is we are free to make decrees that carry the authority of the court of Heaven. Our decrees are based on what is written in the books. Every objection has been removed and the Judge is now free to fulfill His fatherly passion and release His kingdom will in our lives. Nothing is resisting us legally and the decrees now have power.

To get the full effect of this understanding we should look at our position as kings and priests. We are told that we are kings and priests to our God. (Revelation 1:6; Revelation 5:10) This speaks of our spiritual positioning in heaven. These are places given to us by and through the work of Jesus on the cross. The job of a priest is to intercede. The job of a king is to decree. When priests intercede, they grant God the legal right to show mercy. This is most clearly seen in the priest taking the blood into the Holy of Holies on the Day of Atonement. The priest would offer the blood of the Passover lamb in that holy place as prescribed by the Lord. The offering of that blood would grant God the legal right to roll the sins of the people and a nation back for one more year. The Lord by His own mandate needed the function of the priest administrating the blood so He was granted the legalities He needed to bless and show mercy. The job of priest is to strategically intercede so that legal things are in place. Once legal positioning is obtained, then kings, from that place in the spirit, can make decrees. This is why we are to be priests and kings to our God. This is best seen in Jesus coming to Lazarus' tomb in John 11:41-44.

> Then they took away the stone from the place where the dead man was lying. And Jesus lifted up His eyes and said, "Father, I thank You that You have heard Me. And I know that You always hear Me, but because of the people who are standing by I said this, that they may believe that You sent Me." Now when He had said these things, He cried with a loud voice, "Lazarus, come forth!" And he who had died came out bound hand and foot with grave clothes, and his face was wrapped with a cloth. Jesus said to them, "Loose him, and let him go" (John 11:41-44).

Jesus comes to the tomb of Lazarus and says to the Father that He has already prayed. Jesus has been functioning in His priesthood on the journey to Lazarus' tomb. He has dealt with every legal reason why Lazarus has died prematurely. He has been in the courts of Heaven and dealt with the accusations of the devil that allowed Lazarus to die in an untimely fashion. He knows everything is in place legally for what He is about to do. As a result when Jesus comes to Lazarus' tomb, He steps from His priesthood into His kingship. Now He is no longer interceding, now He is decreeing. With authority, He simply decrees, "Lazarus come forth." The dead man rises and comes out of the grave full of life and resurrection power. This is a perfect picture of our function as priest and kings in the courts of Heaven. Once we, from our priesthood, have things legally in place, we can then step into our kingship and make decrees the courts of Heaven back up. Things shift and change in these times by executed verdicts from Heaven put into place.

As we utter the words of governmental decrees, the Heavenly realm is reordered and things come into place for Heaven to invade Earth. There is now a contract and verdict in place from the courts that allows Heaven to manifest on Earth. What a powerful thing! The Holy Spirit will help us in our weakness to maneuver in the courts of Heaven. As we do, we become a part of God's agenda in the planet.

My heart's cry is that this book will help to deal with all the frustration and even skepticism among God's people regarding prayer. I pray that all the prayers that have been prayed in true sincerity but seem to have been unanswered will fade into history as we learn the secrets of the courts. He has not been an uncaring God, or One that is distant. The problem has been that we haven't understood that we must grant God the legal right as Judge to fulfill His fatherly passion. He longs to answer and bless.

We must grant Him the legal right to do so by operating in the courts of Heaven, agreeing with the voices that speak on our behalf and see verdicts rendered from His Throne that establish Kingdom order. When this is done, Heaven will truly invade Earth. Our lives will come to new levels of living, nations will be discipled and Kingdom cultures put into place. There will be an escaping of the destructive schemes of the devil as his legal rights of operation will cease and desist. He will flee at our rebuke because his legal footing has been taken away in the courts of Heaven. Let's move forward and see God's will done. Let's go to court! The verdicts of Heaven are waiting for us.

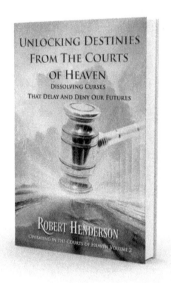

Enjoy
OPERATING IN
THE COURTS OF HEAVEN?

Read
UNLOCKING DESTINIES FROM THE COURTS OF HEAVEN

Robert Henderson is known as a man of revelation and impartation. His teaching on "The Courts of Heaven, The Apostolic, Signs, and Wonders, The Seven Mountains," and numerous other topics, empower people with hidden truths reveled.

With a commission from the Lord to "disciple nations," Robert travels extensively around the globe, fulfilling his mandate. His passion is to see "the knowledge of the glory of the Lord fill the earth, as the waters cover the sea." He believes the best days of nations are yet ahead as the Kingdom of God is expanded in influence. He is on a mission to move the Church from a doomsday mentality to one of raging hope and faith. The God he serves (Jesus) is victorious and always wins!

More great resources from

Robert Henderson

Voice of Reformation

My definition of reformation is the tangible expression of the Kingdom of God in society. One of the greatest challenges facing the Body of Christ is producing the reformers that are necessary to see these mountains re-claimed. When vision is created—intercessors are empowered and reformers are produced and commissioned into their function in these mountains—we will see a living demonstration of the Kingdom of God in Planet Earth through reformation.

The Caused Blessing

When we function in firstfruits, our influence is felt for generations to come, especially throughout our lineage. I always say that if a man's influence only lasts for the span of his natural life, then he is a failure. God intends for our influence to far outlive our natural days. One way this occurs is through the act of firstfruits.

Consecrated Business

Through the principal of firstfruits, businesses can become Kingdom in nature because they are consecrated to the Lord and become holy unto Him. This book will teach you how to birth a Kingdom Business and propel you into a new level of prosperity and influence.

CPSIA information can be obtained
at www.ICGtesting.com
Printed in the USA
LVHW08*2344140818
587027LV00007B/58/P